CREATIVITY

Anthology

MONSIGNOR GLEASON SCHOOL
155 WESTWOOD DRIVE
KITCHENER, ONTARIO

SERIES EDITORS

Margaret Iveson
Samuel Robinson

EDITORIAL CONSULTANT

Alan Simpson

LITERATURE CONSULTANT

Rivka Cranley

TEACHER CONSULTANTS

Janet Hancock
Ian McKay

PRENTICE HALL CANADA INC.

ISBN 0-13-018011-4
© 1993 by Prentice-Hall Canada Inc., Scarborough, Ontario
ALL RIGHTS RESERVED

No part of this book may be reproduced in any form without permission in
writing from the publishers.

Anthologists: Monica Kulling, Todd Mercer
Researchers: Monika Croydon, Catherine Rondina

A Ligature Book
Cover Photograph: Tom Wedell/plasma sphere courtesy of Richard Powers

Canadian Cataloguing in Publication Data
Main entry under title:

Creativity: anthology

(MultiSource)
ISBN 0-13-018011-4

1. Creation (Literary, artistic, etc.)–Literary
collections. 2. Creative ability–Literary collections.
3. Children's literature. I. Iveson, Margaret L., 1948–   .
II. Robinson, Sam, 1937–   . III. Series.
PZ5.C73 1993   j808.8'0353   C92–095393–X

Printed and bound in Canada

Once you commit yourself to "what if,"
anything is possible.

BETTY JANE WYLIE
CANADIAN PLAYWRIGHT

Contents

The Scream

A short story by Diana J. Wieler

Eliza had never been in a drama class. Now that she was here, she was certain it was a mistake. Absolutely certain. There were no desks and no blackboards, no papers or books. The big room was empty, except for a platform at one end, raised eight inches above the shiny hardwood floor. At the other end of the room there were mirrors, a whole wall full, so that you had to see yourself, every time you glanced up.

This isn't going to work! Eliza thought, flattening herself against the wall, her binder clutched over her chest. At thirteen, Eliza wasn't on friendly terms with mirrors. She was too tall and too skinny; her elbows and shoulders stuck out like sharp corners. She was on medication for eczema, but it wasn't helping. No matter what creams or lotions she spread on, her skin was forever white, dry and scaly.

"Lizard skin." Eliza jumped, but no one was even looking at her. Most of the boys and girls were clustered in tight groups in the centre of the room. She knew some of them from last year, grade six.

"This is going to be a blast—no homework or books. Just do plays and stuff. What a cinch!" That was Todd Zudder. Eliza remembered he had pushed her once, in the stairwell at their old school. She had fallen down five stairs.

"So I bumped into her," Todd had shrugged in the principal's office. "I'm clumsy. What can I say?" Eliza was still frightened of stairwells, and Todd Zudder.

"Maybe we can get marks for plays we've already been in," said Melissa Downing. Eliza knew Melissa had already been Baby Bear in The Three Bears, the witch in Hansel and Gretel, and the Snowflake Queen in the grade six Christmas pageant.

How am I going to get out of this? Eliza wondered, her heart thumping. She'd never been in any plays, she'd never even taken baton lessons. How could she cope in this empty room that didn't have any desks? What if they all had to sit on the floor and no one would sit near her?

"Lizard skin." Eliza flinched but pretended she didn't hear. She had practice at pretending like that.

Bang! The chatter stopped abruptly and everyone looked up.

"Thank you," said the teacher, who had slammed the door. "My name is Mrs. Draginda. Don't forget it because I'm not going to write it down. First of all, take off your shoes and set them against the wall."

There were groans and cries of, "Whew! What a stink!" Eliza set down her binder and untied her sneakers with trembling fingers. Did her socks match, did they have any holes? Oh, why hadn't she thought about her socks this morning?

"You will take your shoes off every time you come into this room," Mrs. Draginda said, limping up onto the platform. "I want you to be able to feel the floor under your feet."

One of her legs is shorter than the other, Eliza thought suddenly. It seemed to be what everyone was thinking. Mrs. Draginda looked out at the group with piercing blue eyes.

"I'll tell you two things right now," she said. "I had polio when I was young, so you don't have to ask. And I hate grade sevens. Grade sevens are silly and loud and inhibited." The room started to grumble but Mrs. Draginda cut them off.

"That's right, inhibited. Here's your chance to prove me wrong. Everyone, begin walking in a circle—now!"

It was a command. Eliza leapt up and joined the circle of whispering children. No one had ever met anyone like Mrs. Draginda. They didn't understand her. After all, teachers never came out and said they hated grade sevens. Teachers weren't supposed to hate anybody.

This is going to be awful, Eliza thought numbly, marching around with the rest of them. No desks, no shoes, and a teacher who hated her, right from the start!

"Now, take proud steps. Walk like kings and queens," Mrs. Draginda called. Eliza didn't know how queens walked, but she was pretty sure they didn't leap, the way Melissa Downing was. Melissa was prancing and lunging, a cross between a Snowflake Queen and a swordfighter.

"Don't dance—walk! When I want ballerinas, I'll ask for them."

Melissa stopped leaping, her mouth set in a tight line.

Mrs. Draginda had them walk like kings, then crawl like insects. She had them reach up, as high as they could, then collapse to the floor. Eliza wasn't very good at reaching, but she knew how to fall. She knew the feeling of her arms and legs losing power, she knew what it was like to melt helplessly to the floor in a heap. She did that sometimes when she got home from school, when the door to her room was closed and no one would hear her cry.

Todd Zudder thought collapsing was funny.

"Argh! I'm shot, I'm shot!" he groaned, falling straight forward like a mannequin. Some of the kids laughed.

"Save the theatrics," Mrs. Draginda snapped, "or you'll be doing them out in the hallway—without an audience." The giggles died away.

Eliza was thinking about Mrs. Draginda's limp. At first she'd felt sorry for the teacher, but she didn't now.

No one would make fun of her—they wouldn't dare, Eliza thought. She remembered the icy blue eyes, how they could freeze you where you stood. It'd be a good thing to have eyes like that.

"All right, everyone back in a circle," Mrs. Draginda said, limping into the middle of the room. "We're going to scream."

The class fell silent. Eliza wondered if she'd heard right. What were they going to do?

Mrs. Draginda was in the center of the circle, her arms folded over her chest. She didn't look pleased.

"I told you grade sevens were inhibited," she sighed. "Everyone face inwards. When I point at you, I want you to scream, as loud and hard as you can. No waiting, no pauses, just give me a good primal scream."

She pointed at Todd Zudder. For a moment he was silent, startled, then he broke into a Tarzan yell.

"Out!" Mrs. Draginda jerked her thumb towards the door. "I'll see you after class."

"Hey, wait. I was just . . ."

"Out!" the teacher demanded again, turning her back to him. She pointed at another girl. Todd stomped out and the girl screamed. It was a high, breathy wail, like a starlet in a science fiction movie.

"Next!" Mrs. Draginda cried, cutting her off. One after another the students screamed, each sound flowing into the next as the teacher pointed around the circle.

Eliza was panicking. She had never screamed, not out loud. She couldn't even remember shouting. She had yelled inside her own head a hundred times, but that was different. Now everybody would be watching her, hearing her. The pounding in her ears was so loud it hurt.

"You," Mrs. Draginda said. Eliza closed her eyes. The sound came from the pit of her stomach and tore up through her throat, vibrating in her chest. She could feel something ripping inside her, like a piece of paper being torn in half. It felt good. She pushed in her stomach muscles and the sound went on and on and on until . . .

Silence. Eliza opened her eyes, gasping. Oh no! Everyone was staring at her. Even Mrs. Draginda seemed frozen to the spot, a statue with parted lips. Then she came to life.

"Now that was a scream!" the teacher said. "That's what I want the rest of you to work towards. When I ask you for more, think of that scream."

The teacher stopped talking, but her eyes held Eliza's for a long moment. For the first time, they didn't look cold. The girl felt a warm glow in her stomach, the same place the scream had started.

The class was over too soon. As Eliza pulled on her shoes and picked up her books, she could feel the others watching her. They were whispering; Eliza caught fragments like, "Did you ever?" and "Who would've thought . . ." She knew they weren't talking about her skin or her bony elbows. Eliza stepped out into the hallway, brushing lightly past the surprised face of Todd Zudder.

In Praise of Loneliness

Loneliness of men makes poets.
The great poem is a hymn to loneliness,
a crying out in the night with no ear bent to.

This is a breeding-ground for poets.
Here the spawning, glittering rivers of poetry.
Here is loneliness to live with, sleep with, eat with.
Loneliness of streets, of the coyote.

O Mistress Loneliness, heed your worshipper.
Give him the voice to be heard in this land
Loud with the cluck of the hen and the croak of the frog.

RAYMOND SOUSTER

Future Tense

A short story by Robert Lipsyte

Gary couldn't wait for tenth grade to start so he could strut his sentences, parade his paragraphs, renew his reputation as the top creative writer in school. At the opening assembly, he felt on edge, psyched, like a boxer before the first-round bell. He leaned forward as Dr. Proctor, the principal, introduced two new staff members. He wasn't particularly interested in the new vice-principal, Ms. Jones; Gary never had discipline problems, he'd never even had to stay after school. But his head cocked alertly as Dr. Proctor introduced the new Honors English teacher, Mr. Smith. Here was the person he'd have to impress.

He studied Mr. Smith. The man was hard to describe. He looked as though he'd been manufactured to fit his name. Average height, brownish hair, pale white skin, medium build. Middle age. He was the sort of person you began to forget the minute you met him. Even his clothes had no particular style. They merely covered his body.

Mr. Smith was . . . just there.

Gary was studying Mr. Smith so intently that he didn't hear Dr. Proctor call him up to the stage to receive an award from last term. Jim Baggs jabbed an elbow into his ribs and said, "Let's get up there, Dude."

Dr. Proctor shook Gary's hand and gave him the County Medal for Best Composition. While Dr. Proctor was giving Jim Baggs the County Trophy for Best All-Round Athlete, Gary glanced over his shoulder to see if Mr. Smith looked impressed. But he couldn't find the new teacher. Gary wondered if Mr. Smith was so ordinary he was invisible when no one was talking about him.

On the way home, Dani Belzer, the prettiest poet in school, asked Gary, "What did you think of our new Mr. Wordsmith?"

"If he was a color he'd be beige," said Gary. "If he was a taste he'd be water. If he was a sound he'd be a low hum."

"Fancy, empty words," sneered Mike Chung, ace reporter on the school paper. "All you've told me is you've got nothing to tell me."

Dani quickly stepped between them. "What did you think of the first assignment?"

"Describe a Typical Day at School," said Gary, trying unsuccessfully to mimic Mr. Smith's bland voice. "That's about as exciting as tofu."

"A real artist," said Dani, "accepts the commonplace as a challenge."

That night, hunched over his humming electric typewriter, Gary wrote a description of a typical day at school from the viewpoint of a new teacher who was seeing everything for the very first time, who took nothing for granted. He described the shredded edges of the limp flag outside the dented front door, the worn flooring where generations of kids had nervously paced outside the principal's office, the nauseatingly sweet pipe-smoke seeping out of the teachers' lounge.

And then, in the last line, he gave the composition that extra twist, the little kicker on which his reputation rested. He wrote:

```
The new teacher's beady little eyes
missed nothing, for they were the
optical recorders of an alien creature
who had come to earth to gather infor-
mation.
```

The next morning, when Mr. Smith asked for a volunteer to read aloud, Gary was on his feet and moving toward the front of the classroom before Mike Chung got his hand out of his pocket.

The class loved Gary's composition. They laughed and stamped their feet. Chung shrugged, which meant he couldn't think of any criticism, and Dani flashed thumbs up. Best of all, Jim Baggs shouldered Gary against the blackboard after class and said, "Awesome tale, Dude."

Gary felt good until he got the composition back. Along one margin, in a perfect script, Mr. Smith had written:
You can do better.

"How would he know?" Gary complained on the way home.

"You should be grateful," said Dani. "He's pushing you to the farthest limits of your talent."

"Which may be nearer than you think," snickered Mike.

Gary rewrote his composition, expanded it, complicated it, thickened it. Not only was this new teacher an alien, he was part of an extraterrestrial conspiracy to take over Earth. Gary's final sentence was:

```
Every iota of information, fragment
of fact, morsel of minutiae sucked
up by those vacuuming eyes was beamed
directly into a computer circling the
planet. The data would eventually
become a program that would control
the mind of every school kid on earth.
```

Gary showed the new draft to Dani before class. He stood on tiptoes so he could read over her shoulder. Sometimes he wished she were shorter, but mostly he wished he were taller.

"What do you think?"

"The assignment was to describe a typical day," said Dani. "This is off the wall."

He snatched the papers back. "Creative writing means creating." He walked away, hurt and angry. He thought: *If she doesn't like my compositions, how can I ever get her to like me?*

That morning, Mike Chung read his own composition aloud to the class. He described a typical day through the eyes of a student in a wheelchair. Everything most students take for granted was an obstacle: the bathroom door too heavy to open, the gym steps too steep to climb, the light switch too high on the wall. The class applauded and Mr. Smith nodded approvingly. Even Gary had to admit it was really good—if you considered plain-fact journalism as creative writing, that is.

Gary's rewrite came back the next day marked: *Improving. Try again.*

Saturday he locked himself in his room after breakfast and rewrote the rewrite. He carefully selected his nouns and verbs and adjectives. He polished and arranged them in sentences like a jeweler strings pearls. He felt good as he wrote, as the electric typewriter hummed and buzzed and sometimes coughed. He thought: *Every champion knows that as hard as it is to get to the top, it's even harder to stay up there.*

His mother knocked on his door around noon. When he let her in, she said, "It's a beautiful day."

"Big project," he mumbled. He wanted to avoid a distracting conversation.

She smiled. "If you spend too much time in your room, you'll turn into a mushroom."

He wasn't listening. "Thanks. Anything's okay. Don't forget the mayonnaise."

Gary wrote:

```
The alien's probes trembled as he read
the student's composition. Could that
skinny, bespectacled earthling really
suspect its extraterrestrial identity?
Or was his composition merely the
result of a creative thunderstorm in
a brilliant young mind?
```

Before Gary turned in his composition on Monday morning, he showed it to Mike Chung. He should have known better.

"You're trying too hard," chortled Chung. "Truth is stronger than fiction."

Gary flinched at that. It hurt. It might be true. But he couldn't let his competition know he had scored. "You journalists are stuck in the present and the past," growled Gary. "Imagination prepares us for what's going to happen."

Dani read her composition aloud to the class. It described a typical day from the perspective of a louse choosing a head of hair to nest in. The louse moved from the thicket of a varsity crew-cut to the matted jungle of a sagging perm to a straight, sleek blond cascade.

The class cheered and Mr. Smith smiled. Gary felt a twinge of jealousy. Dani and Mike were coming on. There wasn't room for more than one at the top.

In the hallway, he said to Dani, "And you called my composition off the wall?"

Mike jumped in. "There's a big difference between poetical metaphor and hack science fiction."

Gary felt choked by a lump in his throat. He hurried away.

Mr. Smith handed back Gary's composition the next day marked:

See me after school.

Gary was nervous all day. What was there to talk about? Maybe Mr. Smith hated science fiction. One of those traditional English teachers. Didn't understand that science fiction could be literature. *Maybe I can educate him,* thought Gary.

When Gary arrived at the English office, Mr. Smith seemed nervous too. He kept folding and unfolding Gary's composition. "Where do you get such ideas?" he asked in his monotone voice.

Gary shrugged. "They just come to me."

"Alien teachers. Taking over the minds of school-children." Mr. Smith's empty eyes were blinking. "What made you think of that?"

"I've always had this vivid imagination."

"If you're sure it's just your imagination." Mr. Smith looked relieved. "I guess everything will work out." He handed back Gary's composition. "No more fantasy, Gary. Reality. That's your assignment. Write only about what you know."

Outside school, Gary ran into Jim Baggs, who looked

surprised to see him. "Don't tell me you had to stay after, Dude."

"I had to see Mr. Smith about my composition. He didn't like it. Told me to stick to reality."

"Don't listen." Jim Baggs body checked Gary into the schoolyard fence. "Dude, you got to be yourself."

Gary ran all the way home and locked himself into his room. He felt feverish with creativity. Dude, you got to be yourself, Dude. It doesn't matter what your so-called friends say, or your English teacher. You've got to play your own kind of game, write your own kind of stories.

The words flowed out of Gary's mind and through his fingers and out of the machine and onto sheets of paper. He wrote and rewrote until he felt the words were exactly right:

> With great effort, the alien shut down the electrical panic impulses coursing through its system and turned on Logical Overdrive. There were two possibilities:
>
> 1. This high school boy was exactly what he seemed to be, a brilliant, imaginative, apprentice best-selling author and screenwriter, or,
> 2. He had somehow stumbled onto the secret plan and he would have to be either enlisted into the conspiracy or erased off the face of the planet.

First thing in the morning, Gary turned in his new rewrite to Mr. Smith. A half hour later, Mr. Smith called Gary out of Spanish. There was no expression on his regular features. He said, "I'm going to need some help with you."

Cold sweat covered Gary's body as Mr. Smith grabbed his arm and led him to the new vice-principal. She read the composition while they waited. Gary got a good look at her for the first time. Ms. Jones was . . . just there. She looked as though she'd been manufactured to fit her name. Average. Standard. Typical. The cold sweat turned into goose pimples.

How could he have missed the clues? Smith and Jones were aliens! He had stumbled on their secret and now they'd have to deal with him.

He blurted, "Are you going to enlist me or erase me?"

Ms. Jones ignored him. "In my opinion, Mr. Smith, you are overreacting. This sort of nonsense"—she waved Gary's composition—"is the typical response of an over-stimulated adolescent to the mixture of reality and fantasy in an environment dominated by manipulative music, television, and films. Nothing for us to worry about."

"If you're sure, Ms. Jones," said Mr. Smith. He didn't sound sure.

The vice-principal looked at Gary for the first time. There was no expression in her eyes. Her voice was flat. "You'd better get off this science fiction kick," she said, "If you know what's good for you."

"I'll never tell another human being, I swear," he babbled.

"What are you talking about?" asked Ms. Jones.

"Your secret is safe with me," he lied. He thought, *If I can just get away from them. Alert the authorities. Save the planet.*

"You see," said Ms. Jones, "you're writing yourself into a crazed state."

"You're beginning to believe your own fantasies," said Mr. Smith.

"I'm not going to do anything this time," said

Ms. Jones, "but you must promise to write only about what you know."

"Or I'll have to fail you," said Mr. Smith.

"For your own good," said Ms. Jones. "Writing can be very dangerous."

"Especially for writers," said Mr. Smith, "who write about things they shouldn't."

"Absolutely," said Gary, "positively, no question about it. Only what I know." He backed out the door, nodding in his head, thinking, *Just a few more steps and I'm okay. I hope these aliens can't read minds.*

Jim Baggs was practicing head fakes in the hallway. He slammed Gary into the wall with a hip block. "How's it going, Dude?" he asked, helping Gary up.

"Aliens," gasped Gary. "Told me no more science fiction."

"They can't treat a star writer like that," said Jim. "See what the head honcho's got to say." He grabbed Gary's wrist and dragged him to the principal's office.

"What can I do for you, boys?" boomed Dr. Proctor.

"They're messing with his moves, Doc," said Jim Baggs. "You got to let the aces run their races."

"Thank you, James." Dr. Proctor popped his forefinger at the door. "I'll handle this."

"You're home free, Dude," said Jim, whacking Gary across the shoulder blades as he left.

"From the beginning," ordered Dr. Proctor. He nodded sympathetically as Gary told the entire story, from the opening assembly to the meeting with Mr. Smith and Ms. Jones. When Gary was finished, Dr. Proctor took the papers from Gary's hand. He shook his head as he read Gary's latest rewrite.

"You really have a way with words, Gary. I should have sensed you were on to something."

Gary's stomach flipped. "You really think there could be aliens trying to take over Earth?"

"Certainly," said Dr. Proctor, matter-of-factly. "Earth is the ripest plum in the universe."

Gary wasn't sure if he should feel relieved that he wasn't crazy or be scared out of his mind. He took a deep breath to control the quaver in his voice, and said: "I spotted Smith and Jones right away. They look like they were manufactured to fit their names. Obviously humanoids. Panicked as soon as they knew I was on to them."

Dr. Proctor chuckled and shook his head. "No self-respecting civilization would send those two stiffs to Earth."

"They're not aliens?" He felt relieved and disappointed at the same time.

"I checked them out myself," said Dr. Proctor. "Just two average, standard, typical human beings, with no imagination, no creativity."

"So why'd you hire them?"

Dr. Proctor laughed. "Because they'd never spot an alien. No creative imagination. That's why I got rid of the last vice-principal and the last Honors English teacher. They were giving me odd little glances when they thought I wasn't looking. After ten years on your planet, I've learned to smell trouble."

Gary's spine turned to ice and dripped down the backs of his legs. "You're an alien!"

"Great composition," said Dr. Proctor, waving Gary's papers. "Grammatical, vividly written, and totally accurate."

"It's just a composition," babbled Gary, "made the whole thing up, imagination, you know."

Dr. Proctor removed the face of his wristwatch and

began tapping tiny buttons. "Always liked writers. I majored in your planet's literature. Writers are the keepers of the past and the hope of the future. Too bad they cause so much trouble in the present."

"I won't tell anyone," cried Gary. "Your secret's safe with me." He began to back slowly toward the door.

Dr. Proctor shook his head. "How can writers keep secrets, Gary? It's their natures to share their creations with the world." He tapped three times and froze Gary in place, one foot raised to step out the door.

"But it was only a composition," screamed Gary as his body disappeared before his eyes.

"And I can't wait to hear what the folks back home say when you read it to them," said Dr. Proctor.

"I made it all up." Gary had the sensation of rocketing upward. "I made up the whole . . ."

How Elsa **Became** an Artist

A short story by Mary Alice Thompson

Why Elsa wanted to be an artist, no one knew. But she did want it—more than anything. And so, her mother had arranged for her to have drawing lessons. Once a week Mr. Pole came to their house to look at her sketches and to set new exercises for her. It really seemed that she was making progress . . . until she came upon the sugarshaker.

Mr. Pole said that she needed to work more on drawing simple objects. It was all very well, he said, drawing pictures out of your head of shady ruins and fairies, but you need to learn to work from reality.

So began a long series of exercises in which she would draw cups, a single flower, a book, her own hand. It was terribly boring. But she had to admit that she was learning to look more closely at the things in front of her, and to pay more attention to proportion and shading. Then Mr. Pole told her to find an object with lots of detail and several sides. "Set it in a strong light," he told her, "and pay attention to what the light does."

Elsa found the sugarshaker on a shelf in the basement. It was light, much lighter than one would expect, so that Elsa almost flipped it away when her mother handed it to her.

"I don't know where it came from," Mrs. Tryon said. "It might have been Aunt Betty's. She had a lot of queer old things. Funny that I don't remember it. Anyway, it's got lots of detail for you."

It certainly had. It was silvery and covered in a design of vines and leaves. On its domed top was a crowd of little faces that seemed to be struggling up from the forest below, and from whose eyes, ears and mouths the sugar could be shaken.

Elsa adored it instantly, and carried it off to her room to be set in a strong light and drawn.

Now there was the problem. She spent a very frustrating afternoon. The only way she could describe what was happening was to say that the sugarshaker would not stay still. Every time she looked down at her page to add another line or two to her drawing, she lost sight of the shaker. And then when she looked back, the line wasn't quite where she had seen it before. So she would have to rub it out and start over.

Finally, she stormed out of her room, leaving a desk littered with smudged sketches. Elsa spent the rest of the afternoon playing soccer with Jamie from across the alley, and kicking the ball rather harder than was strictly necessary.

"Geez, Elsa. Take it easy," he protested. "Behind this goofy face lurks a great brain. Don't rattle it."

Elsa laughed. Apart from math, Jamie was an idiot, but he could always make her laugh and she often sought him out. Jamie understood about her wanting to be an artist. He himself wanted to be a composer. He couldn't play an instrument or even sing at all, but Jamie had read everything there was in the library on the physics of music. While other boys listened to Michael Jackson, Jamie was immersed in John Cage. He was Elsa's best friend, but she wasn't ready to explain about the sugar-shaker yet.

"How did your sketching go, Elsa?" her mother asked at dinner.

"Not very well."

"Oh," said her mother. It was understood that it was best not to discuss the subject in detail in front of Dad, who disliked Mr. Pole and disapproved generally of art lessons. But later, her mother came back to the question.

"What's wrong with the sketching, Elsa?"

"Oh—" Elsa fidgeted with the glass she was drying. "—I can't seem to get the details right. I'll try again tomorrow, I guess."

"Don't leave it too long. Mr. Pole is coming Tuesday this week, remember."

Unlike Mr. Tryon, Elsa's mother thought very highly of Mr. Pole. On the whole, Elsa thought she agreed with her dad. Though the teacher had invited her to call him "Fred," she had stuck with "Mr. Pole," feeling decidedly uneasy using the first name of her chilly instructor. Besides, "Pole" suited him so well. He was tall and thin and inflexible. She had once done a cartoon of him, with a flag for a nose. Nevertheless, he was helping her to improve her drawing.

So when she sat down after supper the next night with the sugarshaker in front of her, Elsa tried hard to follow the advice Mr. Pole had given her. She studied the sugarshaker from all sides, idly running her fingers over the little faces, looking for one she thought she remembered but which didn't seem to be there. She counted the sides—nine, which was surely unusual. In some way, holding and touching the sugarshaker pleased her. But again, she could not make a sketch. As she stared at it, the shaker seemed to swim a bit, its surface blurred and writhed, and the little faces on the cap seemed to open and close their mouths like fish.

"I must be tired," Elsa thought, and rubbed her eyes. Finally she gave up and went to bed, puzzled and not a little worried about her mental health.

That night she dreamed about the shaker. In her dream, its surface was still and solid. She could see every detail with almost painful clarity. There, too, was the little face she had lost before, its mouth and eyes open, like a singer producing one clear, piercing note.

She forgot the dream until the next evening when she sat down to sketch. Mr. Pole was coming tomorrow, so she absolutely had to finish the sketch tonight. Staring at the real shaker, she remembered the shaker of her dream and closed her eyes in an effort to recall it. And there it was, imprinted on the back of her eyelids, like a strong light after you stare at it. She opened her eyes and began to sketch, working not from the real shaker but from the one hidden in her dream and inside her eyes.

At lunch the next day she sought out Jamie, although at school they usually went their separate ways.

"It's about this shaker," she said, rolling the bread from her sandwich into pellets. "It's a sugarshaker, which is what people used to use in the old days. And it's—oh, all covered in leaves and has faces at the top. The point is, I keep trying to draw it and I can't. It . . . it doesn't stay still."

"I've always told you you'd never make an artist," said Jamie unsympathetically.

"Oh, please, be serious. I really need to tell someone. The thing is, I did draw it—perfectly. But I had to have this dream about it, and then it stayed still in my mind and I drew it with my eyes shut." She had to explain a couple more times. She knew she wasn't making much sense.

"It's just a clear demonstration of the non-existence of material objects, except as they create sense data. Russell explains it all," Jamie said airily. "You can't really touch a table," he went on. "You just collect sense data."

"But tables don't usually swim and jump around," Elsa reasoned.

"It's like sound," Jamie went on, getting enthusiastic. "You can actually hear a note better when it vibrates—I mean, sound is just vibration anyway. A completely sustained sound would be inaudible. Now about your shaker—"

"Oh, Jamie . . . I haven't a clue what you're driving at. Maybe I should just go home and get it for you, okay?"

The shaker, however, was not where Elsa had left it. Her mother denied knowing anything about it. Before there was time for a thorough search, Mr. Pole arrived. He looked somberly through Elsa's sketches.

"They're not bad; they're actually coming along," he said grudgingly. But he wanted to know if the sugar-shaker had been drawn from life.

"No," Elsa lied, since that seemed easier than trying to explain to Mr. Pole. In any case, what she said was technically true. The shaker had been drawn from her dream.

"Too bad," said Mr. Pole, sounding rather satisfied. "Too bad. It really is an attractive sketch. I might have put it in the art exhibit at the Ex, but if it's only imaginary . . . " Then he shook himself like a dog and went on with the lesson.

That night Elsa searched the house from top to bottom for the sugarshaker, but she couldn't find it anywhere.

"Perhaps it never existed," said Jamie cheerfully, when she opened the newest aspect of her problem to him the next day.

"Well, I wish it had," said Elsa, "because I'd like to be in that art show. I'm thirteen already and I haven't shown anything. Do you know, I'll bet Picasso had a one-man show at fifteen. How am I ever going to match that?"

"It's tough getting your first break, all right," Jamie agreed. "I gave my mom a choice last night—music lessons, or a computer. And do you know what she said? Neither one. She says I'm just going through a phase. It's going to be a short one if I don't get some encouragement soon."

They sat together glumly for a while, and then played a rather directionless game of soccer.

That night Elsa pursued her one remaining clue.

"Mom, tell me about Aunt Betty."

"Oh, well, there's not much to tell. She was your great-grandfather's sister, or half-sister, I think. She had polio as a child, and I believe it disfigured her quite badly. Anyway, she lived in a home. A few years ago we got a letter from her lawyer saying that we were her last living relatives, and that she wanted us to have her remaining effects. I think she's still alive, but wandering in her mind, you know. I threw most of the stuff out, I'm afraid. It was junk—old books and trinkets. I kept some of the photos, though, and the china. Funny I don't remember that sugarshaker."

"What sort of books were they?"

"Oh, spiritualism," said her mother briskly. "Animal magnetism, hypnotism—nonsense like that."

Elsa went into the basement and found the box with Aunt Betty's things. But the contents were disappointing

—some pretty but chipped china, a silver-backed mirror and brush, and a box of old photographs. At first, Elsa felt some excitement about the pictures, but as she went through them her disappointment grew. Mountains, lakes, trees, a few horses—that was all. There were no people, and certainly no sugarshaker.

Elsa might have forgotten the whole affair had she not been so determined to have her sketch shown at the Ex. She spoke to her mother, who had a quiet word with Mr. Pole, and the sketch was entered. A few days later came the news that she had won first prize for her age in the black and white category. She would get her ribbon in the mail. Elsa was thrilled, but she was even more eager to see her work on display. So on Saturday, she and Jamie made plans to go together.

At the Ex, Elsa pretended some interest in the rides and the games, but Jamie, like the good friend he was, insisted on going straight to the pavilion where the arts and crafts were displayed. They wandered past tables of jams and needlepoint to the area where the art was on show. And there was Elsa's sketch of the sugarshaker, complete with a red ribbon.

"It's a small start," she said to Jamie, "but gratifying." Really, she was immensely proud, and had to keep reminding herself that it was a long way from a one-man show, just to keep from floating away.

They went back to the midway and glutted themselves with junk food and rides. Jamie wanted to see the display on technology, but Elsa soon lost interest. Jamie was morosely contemplating the computer on which he would compose his masterpiece, and Elsa sensed that her own irrepressible buoyance was irritating. They agreed to meet later for the grandstand show.

Elsa found herself drifting back to the arts and crafts

pavilion. She amused herself by watching the crowd, many of whom were dressed in costumes of the 1890s for the exhibition celebrating the Klondike gold rush. It was no surprise to her, then, to see a woman in a long dress standing before her picture. As she drew closer, the woman spoke without turning around.

"You did a very nice job of it, my dear. That's just what it looked like."

She could be addressing no one but Elsa, so Elsa replied, somewhat hesitantly, "Thank you."

"And now," said the woman, turning around with a smile, "you must draw me." The face was gentle and friendly, though it was hard to guess what age she might be.

"I haven't started portraiture yet," said Elsa, trying to be polite. It seemed rude to demand outright who the woman might be. Elsa had the strangest feeling that—but no, it wasn't possible. Aunt Betty, if she were still alive, would be over a hundred. And in a wheelchair. And in Scotland.

"I don't mean to startle you, Elsa," said the woman. Did she have an accent? "I owe you some explanations, I know. Shall we sit over here?" She led Elsa to a bench nearby. "I don't know how long I can stay."

"Who are you?" Elsa asked, her curiosity getting the better of her.

"I am your grandfather's—no, great-grandfather's half-sister, Elizabeth. We were only a year apart, you know, Jimmy and I, and when we were young we were very close. He wanted to be a sailor, and I was going to be a horse-woman. We used to joke about how we would sail around the world to all the equestrian meets." She laughed. "I'm afraid some of them were quite far inland. We knew so little then." She had wonderful black eyes that sparkled and opened wide. "My horse was called Tobacco."

"And the sugarshaker?" asked Elsa tentatively. "It was yours?"

"Oh, yes. It was very dear to me. I grew up with it and loved its little faces. Father disapproved of sugar on oatmeal, you know, but Mother always let us use it. But I lost it, you see, the same summer that I lost . . . the summer I had polio. It was on the kitchen table the morning I felt ill and went back to bed. Months later, when I was finally strong enough to be carried downstairs, it was gone. No one knew what had become of it. I cried for it like a little child."

"But you found it again."

"Oh, no. It was never found."

"But then—"

"Oh, my dear, there is so much to explain, and I don't know how long I can stay. The sugarshaker that you had . . . I made it and sent it to you. You see, for many years now I've been wandering in my mind, and finally I found you, and you seemed so sympathetic that it gave me an idea. I used to do a lot of reading, my dear, before I . . . well, retired. And so I sent you the sugarshaker, just as an experiment, to see if it would work. I had a hard time remembering all the details, so it was a bit . . . loose . . . at first. But you are wonderful, Elsa, truly. You grasped it all, and met me halfway. You saw it, and drew it, just as it really was."

"But why didn't my mother notice that it was, well, loose?"

"She probably never really looked at it. So few people do."

"And now it's gone."

"Well, really, you know, it was gone a long time ago. What you had was only there as long as I sustained it for you. It really is very hard work."

"And you? I mean . . . right now?"

"Quite right, my dear. You really are most acute. It's very tiring, just staying here."

"And you want me to draw you?"

"It's vain of me, isn't it? I don't suppose I ever looked quite like this, but this is how I always pictured myself. I know I'm still a bit blurry, but I'm steadier than the shaker." Here she laughed gently, almost musically.

"You see," Betty went on, "I'm one hundred and five. I have no family but you. I could never have lovers or children, and my dear Jimmy left when he knew there was no hope for him at home, and no hope for me anywhere. Actually, I made him go. He would have wasted his whole life hanging around me. But I'm wandering. The point is, I want to leave something, something of what I might have been, behind me." She sounded so sad, and yet she smiled and her eyes shone.

"So you will draw me, won't you? As I am now?"

"I'll try!" cried Elsa, and impulsively kissed her.

"That makes me so happy," Betty whispered, though Elsa often wondered afterwards if she meant the kiss or the consent.

"And now," said Betty, standing up, "it must be time for you to meet your friend. I'll visit you again, for the portrait. Right now, I'm just going to look at the sugar-shaker again. I really was very fond of it. Goodbye," she said softly, and blew Elsa a kiss.

"Goodbye," said Elsa, and watched her move back into the crowd.

Checking her watch, Elsa saw that she was late for her rendezvous with Jamie, and set off sprinting to the appointed place.

She arrived, out of breath, to find Jamie in a much better mood, bubbling over with all he had learned at the technology display. As they walked to the grandstand, Elsa could hardly hear him, her mind being wholly taken up with her own eventful afternoon. Jamie was explaining about holograms when suddenly he caught Elsa's attention.

"It's like seeing, maybe even touching, a thing that doesn't exist," he explained. "Like speaking mind to mind, without words."

Elsa was very alert.

"Could you do it without the computer?" she demanded.

"I don't know," Jamie considered. "I suppose you could say that that's what a musician or an artist does all the time."

Elsa spent every day after that in anticipation of a visit from Betty. School was over now, and she occupied her days sketching madly. Jamie had agreed to let her do his portrait, and she did a creditable job. She had not yet dared to show it to Mr. Pole, who had told her sourly that she was not ready for portraiture and not to let her success at the Ex go to her head.

As the summer wore on, Elsa accumulated an impressive file of secret portraits—several of Jamie, a few self-portraits, portraits of strangers in the park, and even one of her mother done while she was watching television and unaware what Elsa was sketching. But still Betty did not come.

She thought afterwards that she should have known how Betty would appear. She came in Elsa's dream one night and stood in a green meadow, wearing a funny brown suit, her hand raised in an odd gesture or salute. She chattered away in her light manner, but Elsa could not quite make out what she said. Still, she could see her very clearly.

Elsa awoke from the dream in the middle of the night with every detail so firmly in her mind that she had to start drawing immediately. She sketched fluently, without hesitation, every fold of the suit, every shadow of the face. But when she was finished, there seemed to be something wrong about the sketch . . . something was missing. At dawn she went back to bed, exhausted.

"Elsa," said her mother a few days later, "would you like to see if we can find a new drawing teacher?"

Elsa looked up inquisitively. Mother had always been so stuck on Mr. Pole. This change was surprising.

"I didn't mean to pry, Elsa," she went on, "but I couldn't help seeing the portrait you made of the lady in a riding habit, and it really made me think that you might have outgrown Mr. Pole."

Elsa was overjoyed, not only for the release from Mr. Pole, to which she emphatically assented, but even more for the casual information her mother had provided. The funny suit was a riding habit! Now she knew why the portrait had felt incomplete.

Elsa went down to the basement to find the stack of photographs. She now saw that what she had at first thought were several different horses was, in fact, one horse. She felt sure this was Tobacco. Elsa chose a picture with the pose she needed and returned upstairs to the portrait of Betty. Paying careful attention to the light and detail, she drew in the horse, his neck under the raised hand that had previously seemed meaningless. Its message was not, after all, a half-hearted goodbye but a caress.

School started the next day. Elsa walked home with Jamie, discussing teachers, classmates and prospects for the new year. She went to his house to see the new trumpet that his mother had finally been badgered into giving him.

"It's cheaper than a computer," he explained, "and

she thinks it will make me more sociable if I play in the band. She's right, I think," he added. "I was in real danger of becoming a recluse this summer. I've been reading Aristotle, and I'm convinced that man's true nature is political. I think I shall have to lead a more active, useful life. Also, I discovered this incredible program while you were buried in your sketchbook. It's called 'Two New Hours,' and it's fantastic. Why did nobody tell me about it? It's on CBC radio, and it's probably going to be cut now that I've discovered it. I'm going to write a letter to my MP about the cuts to the CBC." Which he did.

Elsa called the drawing of Betty *Portrait of a Horse-woman* and entered it in a contest for an art scholarship. And in the same post that brought a letter to her father saying that Miss Elizabeth Melville of Dundee was deceased and had left just enough to cover her funeral expenses, came a letter to Elsa herself, telling her that her tuition to art school would be paid.

PAINTING
Rocks

From the novel *In Summer Light*
by Zibby Oneal

The beach was small and, for a Saturday, there weren't many people there. Mostly there were children digging in the clay. A few couples sunned themselves like seals on rocks near the water. Kate leaned back on her towel and closed her eyes and felt the sun on her forehead and eyelids.

"Are we going to paint rocks?" Ian said.

"Do you really want to?"

"I thought that was the reason we came to this beach."

"We'll feel silly."

"Why should we?"

"It's something children do."

"Until now, maybe." He tugged her hand. "Come on. You said you loved it."

Well, and she *had* loved it, a long time ago, but she stood up, half-reluctant.

"You'll have to show me how you do it," Ian said.

Kate made a face at him. "I think you can probably figure it out."

A couple lying side by side propped up and watched them walk toward the water. Then they lay back down, oblivious. Ian stooped at the water's edge and scraped up a great dripping handful of clay. "Here goes," he said, and began to smear clay on the nearest boulder. Kate took her time, looking for a rock with a smooth surface.

She remembered having done this countless times. While the other children plunged in and began to smear clay, she had held back, studying the rocks critically, searching for one whose surface was right. She walked slowly along the shore now, searching. Half-remembering, she made her way to the end of the beach, to the point where the cliffs rose straight out of the water. And there was the rock. Its sheared face fronted on the sea, smoothed by who-knew-how-many years of weathering. It towered above her, enormous still, although she was many times taller than she had been the last time she tried to paint it. Its sheer face was like a wall but she remembered that on its back side there were footholds. She remembered it suddenly in great detail.

For a minute she stood looking at the rock's face, remembering the effort it had taken to work her way even halfway up, and then she scooped up a handful of clay and made a first great swooping curve low down on the smooth surface. The warm rock and the dripping clay and the itch of sand on her palm were so familiar that she might have been nine years old again; nothing changed. And then Kate remembered that the last time she painted the rock she had been twelve, and that she had ruined a new bikini, staining it with clay. She supposed that she had ruined all her bathing suits the years she painted rocks.

She looked down at the suit she wore and thought that she ought to have warned Ian about the lasting effects of the clay on cloth. But then she went back to painting.

She made a series of curves, scooping clay and sweeping it higher on the rock, using the palms of her hands and her fingers like brushes. Water lapped her ankles and the red clay ran down her arms, streaking her with red. She scooped and painted, laying down great overlapping strokes, interlocking curves, spiraling patterns. She did a series of snail whorls that she remembered having seen on a Cretan vase. Then a sort of free-form octopus shape. Shapes and patterns came to her from pictures she'd looked at, from pottery she'd seen in glass cases in echoing museum rooms. She forgot to look around at Ian. She began not to hear the voices of the children on the beach.

Scooping and painting, she made her way around the rock to the rougher side, carried by the momentum of the curving shapes she was painting. The bulging outcroppings of the rock began to dictate shapes to her, and like a cave painter, she began to use these as part of her design. A swoop here. A zigzag there. A free sweep of clay down a crevice. She stood on tiptoe, stretching as far as she could, and made a fat bulge of rock above her into the side of a bison. Clay ran down her body, drying and caking in the wind. She left her own handprints on the rock, as the ancient painters at Lascaux had done.

Finally she had gone as far as she could without climbing. She tipped back her head and looked up. The old footholds were still there—naturally occurring indentations in the rock, just as she remembered them. She scooped handfuls of clay and flung them at the rock above her, spattering herself with red. She scooped and threw until there were mounds of clay clinging to the outcroppings—enough, she judged, to finish the painting. And then she hoisted herself and began to climb.

It felt wonderful climbing up into the wind. Her hair snapped against her shoulders. Her feet searched the rock for holds. Her toes dug in, and the rough stone pressed hard against her soles. Her whole body became a brush, bending to scoop the clay she'd thrown. She smeared it in great free whirls across the rock, working her way toward the top.

Far below her, she could see Ian, the couples sunning themselves beside the water, the children running on the sand. She hoisted herself to the top of the rock and clung there, looking far out over the water. She had never made it to the top before. She had never been tall enough before to pull herself up the last several feet.

She felt triumphant. She wanted to keep climbing, to keep painting, to go on and on painting her way into the layers of blue above her. And then she stood up, digging her toes in, balancing on the uneven surface. The wind whipped her hair into streamers behind her. Her eyes stung, but she felt wonderful. She stood fighting the wind like a flag.

Below her, Ian looked up. She waved to him. She waved to the couples on the rocks, semaphoring with her red-stained arms. She wanted to yell. She wanted to make the wild, hoarse, screaming sounds the gulls made. And then, quite suddenly, she wanted to fly.

She leapt straight out, pushing off hard with her feet, and for a minute it felt like flying. She felt herself plummeting down through the air, and the wind whistling past her. The sand rose toward her. She saw Ian running. She landed. A perfect landing, in a crouch, both feet firmly in the sand.

"My God!" Ian said, "Were you trying to kill yourself?"

Kate rolled over, laughing, in the sand. "No," she said, "I was flying."

Her legs, her arms, her whole body were dyed red and encrusted with sand. Her hair was stiff with clay. She jumped up and began running toward the water. "Come on," she called over her shoulder, "wash off."

She dived into a wave, shot up on the other side. She swam hard a few yards, still feeling the wild, free-fall of her body cutting through thin air. Clay streamed off her just as she remembered. The water around her turned red.

"It never all comes off," she said. "We'll be a little bit this color for a day or two. I forgot to tell you that."

Ian was drying off, streaking the towel. Kate looked at her rock with satisfaction. The clay was nearly dry. Her swoops and curves looked ancient, as if they had been there as long as the rock had.

Ian stretched out on the towel beside her. Kate contentedly poured handfuls of sand over her feet. "Why did you jump off that rock?" he said.

"Felt like it."

"It wasn't a very smart thing to do."

"No," she agreed. She supposed that was true. But she remembered the pure feeling of joy as she sailed through the air, her body like an extension of the curves she had painted.

"Well, you did some nice things with the rock," he said, "anyway."

Kate studied the rock. "I kept remembering things I'd seen," she said. "Pictures of cave paintings, pottery designs, all kinds of things." She stretched out her legs and looked at her toes. "Right now I wish I could spend my whole life painting rocks," she said.

"What about just painting?"

Kate glanced at him, lying flat, eyes closed. He was serious. "That's what my father does," she said.

"That's what a lot of people do."

"No, Ian," she said, "I told you a long time ago, I need my own thing."

"Does painting stop being a person's 'own thing' just because other people are also painting?"

"No, of course."

"Well, then?"

Kate curled her toes and said nothing.

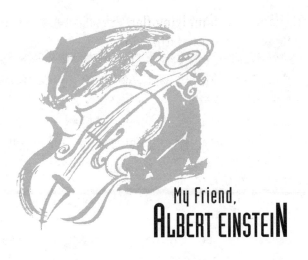

My Friend,
ALBERT EINSTEIN

An essay by Banesh Hoffmann

He was one of the greatest scientists the world has ever known, yet if I had to convey the essence of Albert Einstein in a single word, I would choose *simplicity*. Perhaps an anecdote will help. Once, caught in a downpour, he took off his hat and held it under his coat. Asked why, he explained, with admirable logic, that the rain would damage the hat, but his hair would be none the worse for its wetting. This knack for going instinctively to the heart of a matter was the secret of his major scientific discoveries—this and his extraordinary feeling for beauty.

I first met Albert Einstein in 1935, at the famous Institute for Advanced Study in Princeton, N.J. He had been among the first to be invited to the Institute, and was offered *carte blanche*[1] as to salary. To the director's dismay, Einstein asked for an impossible sum: it was far

[1] **carte blanche** [kärt blänsh´]: French for "blank check"; unrestricted freedom of action.

too *small*. The director had to plead with him to accept a larger salary.

I was in awe of Einstein, and hesitated before approaching him about some ideas I had been working on. When I finally knocked on his door, a gentle voice said, "Come"—with a rising inflection that made the single word both a welcome and a question. I entered his office and found him seated at a table, calculating and smoking his pipe. Dressed in ill-fitting clothes, his hair characteristically awry, he smiled a warm welcome. His utter naturalness at once set me at ease.

As I began to explain my ideas, he asked me to write the equations on the blackboard so he could see how they developed. Then came the staggering—and altogether endearing—request: "Please go slowly. I do not understand things quickly." This from Einstein! He said it gently, and I laughed. From then on, all vestiges of fear were gone.

Einstein was born in 1879 in the German city of Ulm. He had been no infant prodigy; indeed, he was so late in learning to speak that his parents feared he was a dullard. In school, though his teachers saw no special talent in him, the signs were already there. He taught himself calculus, for example, and his teachers seemed a little afraid of him because he asked questions they could not answer. At the age of 16, he asked himself whether a light wave would seem stationary if one ran abreast of it. From that innocent question would arise, ten years later, his theory of relativity.[2]

Einstein failed his entrance examinations at the Swiss Federal Polytechnic School, in Zurich, but was admitted a year later. There he went beyond his regular work to study the masterworks of physics on his own. Rejected

[2] **theory of relativity:** Einstein's theory concerning the relationship among matter, energy, space, time, and gravitation

when he applied for academic positions, he ultimately found work, in 1902, as a patent examiner in Berne,[3] and there in 1905 his genius burst into fabulous flower.

Among the extraordinary things he produced in that memorable year were his theory of relativity, with its famous offshoot, $E = mc^2$ (energy equals mass times the speed of light squared), and his quantum theory of light.[4] These two theories were not only revolutionary, but seemingly contradictory: the former was intimately linked to the theory that light consists of waves, while the latter said it consists somehow of particles. Yet this unknown young man boldly proposed both at once—and he was right in both cases, though how he could have been is far too complex a story to tell here.

Collaborating with Einstein was an unforgettable experience. In 1937, the Polish physicist Leopold Infeld and I asked if we could work with him. He was pleased with the proposal, since he had an idea about gravitation waiting to be worked out in detail. Thus we got to know not merely the man and the friend, but also the professional.

The intensity and depth of his concentration were fantastic. When battling a recalcitrant problem, he worried it as an animal worries its prey. Often, when we found ourselves up against a seemingly insuperable difficulty, he would stand up, put his pipe on the table, and say in his quaint English, "I will a little tink" (he could not pronounce "th"). Then he would pace up and down, twirling a lock of his long, graying hair around his forefinger.

A dreamy, faraway and yet inward look would come over his face. There was no appearance of concentration, no furrowing of the brow—only a placid inner communion.

---

[3] **Berne:** city in Switzerland
[4] **quantum** [kwon′təm] **theory of light:** Originally set forth by the German physicist Max Planck (1858–1947), quantum theory states that radiant energy, like light, is transmitted in separate units rather than in a continuous stream.

The minutes would pass, and then suddenly Einstein would stop pacing as his face relaxed into a gentle smile. He had found the solution to the problem. Sometimes it was so simple that Infeld and I could have kicked ourselves for not having thought of it. But the magic had been performed invisibly in the depths of Einstein's mind, by a process we could not fathom.

Although Einstein felt no need for religious ritual and belonged to no formal religious group, he was the most deeply religious man I have known. He once said to me, "Ideas come from God," and one could hear the capital "G" in the reverence with which he pronounced the word. On the marble fireplace in the mathematics building at Princeton University is carved, in the original German, what one might call his scientific credo: "God is subtle, but he is not malicious." By this Einstein meant that scientists could expect to find their task difficult, but not hopeless: the Universe was a Universe of law, and God was not confusing us with deliberate paradoxes[5] and contradictions.

Einstein was an accomplished amateur musician. We used to play duets, he on the violin, I at the piano. One day he surprised me by saying Mozart was the greatest composer of all. Beethoven "created" his music, but the music of Mozart was of such purity and beauty one felt he had merely "found" it—that it had always existed as part of the inner beauty of the Universe, waiting to be revealed.

It was this very Mozartean simplicity that most characterized Einstein's methods. His 1905 theory of relativity, for example, was built on just two simple assumptions. One is the so-called principle of relativity, which means,

---

[5] **paradoxes:** A paradox is anything that is itself seemingly inconsistent or contradictory. Some paradoxes, although apparently absurd, ultimately prove true.

roughly speaking, that we cannot tell whether we are at rest or moving smoothly. The other assumption is that the speed of light is the same no matter what the speed of the object that produces it. You can see how reasonable this is if you think of agitating a stick in a lake to create waves. Whether you wiggle the stick from a stationary pier, or from a rushing speedboat, the waves, once generated, are on their own, and their speed has nothing to do with that of the stick.

Each of these assumptions, by itself, was so plausible as to seem primitively obvious. But together they were in such violent conflict that a lesser man would have dropped one or the other and fled in panic. Einstein daringly kept both—and by so doing he revolutionized physics. For he demonstrated they could, after all, exist peacefully side by side, provided we gave up cherished beliefs about the nature of time.

Science is like a house of cards, with concepts like time and space at the lowest level. Tampering with time brought most of the house tumbling down, and it was this that made Einstein's work so important—and controversial. At a conference in Princeton in honor of his 70th birthday, one of the speakers, a Nobel Prize-winner, tried to convey the magical quality of Einstein's achievement. Words failed him, and with a shrug of helplessness he pointed to his wristwatch, and said in tones of awed amazement, "It all came from this." His very ineloquence made this the most eloquent tribute I have heard to Einstein's genius.

We think of Einstein as one concerned only with the deepest aspects of science. But he saw scientific principles in everyday things to which most of us would give barely a second thought. He once asked me if I had ever wondered why a man's feet will sink into either dry or completely submerged sand, while sand that is merely damp provides a firm surface. When I could not answer, he offered a simple explanation.

It depends, he pointed out, on *surface tension,* the elastic-skin effect of a liquid surface. This is what holds a drop together, or causes two small raindrops on a windowpane to pull into one big drop the moment their surfaces touch.

When sand is damp, Einstein explained, there are tiny amounts of water between grains. The surface tensions of these tiny amounts of water pull all the grains together, and friction then makes them hard to budge. When the sand is dry, there is obviously no water between grains. If the sand is fully immersed, there is water between grains, but no water *surface* to pull them together.

This is not as important as relativity; yet there is no telling what seeming trifle will lead an Einstein to a major discovery. And the puzzle of the sand does give us an inkling of the power and elegance of his mind.

Einstein's work, performed quietly with pencil and paper, seemed remote from the turmoil of everyday life: But his ideas were so revolutionary they caused violent controversy and irrational anger. Indeed, in order to be able to award him a belated Nobel Prize, the selection committee had to avoid mentioning relativity, and pretend the prize was awarded primarily for his work on the quantum theory.

Political events upset the serenity of his life even more. When the Nazis came to power in Germany, his theories were officially declared false because they had been formulated by a Jew. His property was confiscated, and it is said a price was put on his head.

When scientists in the United States, fearful that the Nazis might develop an atomic bomb, sought to alert

American authorities to the danger, they were scarcely heeded. In desperation, they drafted a letter which Einstein signed and sent directly to President Roosevelt. It was this act that led to the fateful decision to go all-out on the production of an atomic bomb—an endeavor in which Einstein took no active part. When he heard of the agony and destruction that his $E = mc^2$ had wrought, he was dismayed beyond measure, and from then on there was a look of ineffable sadness in his eyes.

There was something elusively whimsical about Einstein. It is illustrated by my favorite anecdote about him. In his first year in Princeton, on Christmas Eve, so the story goes, some children sang carols outside his house. Having finished, they knocked on his door and explained they were collecting money to buy Christmas presents. Einstein listened, then said, "Wait a moment." He put on his scarf and overcoat, and took his violin from its case. Then, joining the children as they went from door to door, he accompanied their singing of "Silent Night" on his violin.

How shall I sum up what it meant to have known Einstein and his works? Like the Nobel Prize-winner who pointed helplessly at his watch, I can find no adequate words. It was akin to the revelation of great art that lets one see what was formerly hidden. And when, for example, I walk on the sand of a lonely beach, I am reminded of his ceaseless search for cosmic simplicity—and the scene takes on a deeper, sadder beauty.

CHAGALL

A one-act play by Rick McNair

CHARACTERS

MARC CHAGALL

OLD CHAGALL, referred to as CHAGALL

YOUNG CHAGALL 1; YOUNG CHAGALL 2; YOUNG
    CHAGALL 3; YOUNG CHAGALL 4—who represent
    aspects of Old Chagall's subconscious

MOTHER of Marc Chagall

FATHER of Marc Chagall

TEACHERS: TEACHER 1; TEACHER 2

KIDS: GIRL; TOUGH KID 1; TOUGH KID 2

PHOTOGRAPHER

HUSBAND; WIFE; four children

PENNE, the art teacher

RINGMASTER 1; RINGMASTER 2; RINGMASTER 3;
    RINGMASTER 4; RINGMASTER 5

CIRCUS PERFORMERS: Petrov Georgi; The Georgi
    Family; elephants; female tightrope walker

BELLA, a smiling young woman

Guest at the wedding
Relative at the wedding
Distant Cousin at the wedding
Hupah Holder
Rabbi
Accuser 1; Accuser 2; Accuser 3; Accuser 4
Russian Official

Stage Setting: *The setting for the entire play is a circus. There should be about five round platforms of various sizes to stand or sit on. They will serve as tables and chairs. Colored ladders and a monkey bar could be centre stage. Everything should be painted in the vibrant colors characteristic of Chagall's paintings.*

(Old Chagall *enters and takes a blue handkerchief and turns it red.*)

Chagall. I would paint all of that (*pointing to something in the theatre*) the brightest red I could make. And over there I would have a small house with walls that bend a little, and on its roof would be an old man. He looks a little like me. He'd sit on a rocking chair and eat carrots. And there . . . no . . . more to the left, there would be a giant violin, or fiddle, or what-you-will. And right there would be a purple cow. Yes, mooing in its own color. A rooster there, and a yellow fish there. And all the space in between will be blue, with stars living in it. I'll paint people everywhere. Some will walk, and some will fly . . . maybe we could even see through some of them. Some things look better upside down. And over there I will have an angel. The whole place will be my circus. Excuse me, I am being rude. I have forgotten to introduce myself. My name is Marc . . . Chagall. I paint pictures, make rugs, pots, colored glass windows. Some people tell me I'm the most famous painter in the world. I bet you never heard of me or, if you did, you probably can't remember . . . But that's all right. I can't even remember when I was born. Let me see . . . it was 1887 . . . or was it 1889? Well, it doesn't matter. But I do remember I always wanted to be a painter. (YOUNG CHAGALL 1, YOUNG CHAGALL 2, *and* YOUNG CHAGALL 3 *enter, dressed alike.*)

YOUNG CHAGALL 1. When I grow up, I'm going to be . . .

CHAGALL. I remember I said . . .

YOUNG CHAGALL 1. . . . a violinist.

YOUNG CHAGALL 2. What are you going to be?

YOUNG CHAGALL 1. A fiddler!

YOUNG CHAGALL 3. When you grow up?

CHAGALL and YOUNG CHAGALL 1. A fiddler!

YOUNG CHAGALL 2. That's not a real job.

YOUNG CHAGALL 1. I'll study at the Academy of Music.

CHAGALL. My fiddle will make the stars dance. Yes, I wanted to be a violinist as well. A magic sound.

YOUNG CHAGALL 3. I am going to be a poet.

YOUNG CHAGALL 1. What?

YOUNG CHAGALL 3. To write words upon the wind . . . to spill magic from my heart . . . to make ink dance on a field of white.

CHAGALL. Yes—a poet! I'll study to be a . . .
(YOUNG CHAGALL 4 *enters, singing.*)

YOUNG CHAGALL 4. Singer. I want to sing out loud, let notes float to the sky.

CHAGALL (*singing a scale with the letters of his name*).
C-H-A-G-A-L-L, Chagall! I want to be a . . .

YOUNG CHAGALL 2. A dancer. To dance across the roofs, to leap, to float, to fly! (*He dances but he falls.*)

YOUNG CHAGALL 3. To sink.

CHAGALL. I want to be a . . .

YOUNG CHAGALL 1, 2, 3, and 4. Fiddler, poet, singer, dancer.
(*The four young* CHAGALLS *exit, arguing.*)

CHAGALL. A painter. Maybe I did want to be a lot of different things. Clowns and acrobats and bareback riders too. They all still sound like fun.
(MARC, *as a young boy, and his mother enter.*)

MOTHER. I have got you into school. It hasn't been easy.

CHAGALL. She had to bribe the school to take me. Not everyone was allowed to go to school then. Not such a bad idea you think?

MOTHER. Marc, sit down over there, learn as much as you can, and you will get a good job . . . a clerk perhaps. Now don't be frightened.
(MARC *does as he is told and* MOTHER *exits.*)

CHAGALL. She got me into school for better or worse. What can I say about my mother? We loved each other; we disappointed each other; we needed each other. Maybe all I can say is . . . tears.
(*The kids enter.* TEACHER 1 *and* TEACHER 2 *enter, one on each side of* MARC.)

TEACHER 1. Marc Chagall, sit there.
(MARC *sits on one of the round platforms.*)

TEACHER 2. Take this book.

TEACHER 1. Put your name in it.

TEACHER 2. Today we will study the names of the czars . . .

TEACHER 1. . . . and czarinas . . .

TEACHER 2. . . . of all of Russia.

TEACHERS. Ivan, Peter, Alexander, Ivan, Nicholas, Catherine, Ivan, Ivan, and more Ivans. Ivan, Alexander, and Anne.

MARC (*not paying attention to the teachers*). Name —Marc Chagall. Address—Pokrowsskaja Street. The Town of Vitebsk. Russia. Europe. Northern

Hemisphere. The World. The Solar System. The Milky Way. The Universe. Infinity.

TEACHER 1. Marc Chagall, name five Russian czars.

MARC. Um . . . Al, no, Al . . . Fred? . . . Um.

TEACHERS. Don't know them, eh?

TEACHER 1. Two black marks for bad behavior.

TEACHER 2. Bad behavior.

(**TEACHERS 1** *and* **2** *exit.*)

CHAGALL. I really did know them. I wasn't going to say them out loud. To me, history smelled too dead. It was just lists of dead czars. But . . . geometry . . .

KIDS. Geometry!

CHAGALL. It was magic signs and shapes that flew through space.

(*Throughout the following verses, various designs and shapes are made with a large loop of material. At least four students are involved in a kind of a giant cat and cradle game. A large six-point star is the final result.*)

KIDS. Dots are moving to form two lines.
Parallel line, they never touch.
All in the circle I say is mine.
Ninety degrees is much too much.
Circle, Line, Triangle, Square,
You can make them anywhere.
With your compass draw what you will,
Make a perfect star and hold it still.
Round and round the magic star goes,
Where it stops nobody knows.

CHAGALL. I liked geometry. I also liked girls.

GIRL. Hello.

MARC. Hello.

CHAGALL. I had rosy cheeks and I was cute. I couldn't help myself.

GIRL. I'm better now.

MARC. You look better.

CHAGALL. She had freckles. Do angels have freckles? Oh, I bet some of them do.

GIRL. I don't have the measles anymore.

MARC. Did they hurt?

GIRL. Not much.

MARC. Was it my fault you had the measles?

GIRL. How?

MARC. Because I kissed you?

GIRL. No, silly!

MARC. I can do it again . . . and I will. (*He does.*)

TOUGH KID 1. Hey! Who said you could do that?

CHAGALL. She did.

TOUGH KID 1. Where do you think you're going?

TOUGH KID 2. Yeah. Where do you think you're going?

MARC (trying to sneak away). Oh . . . nowhere. (*He stops.*)

TOUGH KID 1. Are you trying to get tough with me?

TOUGH KID 2. Trying to get tough with me?

MARC. No.

TOUGH KID 1. You're the kid who paints.

MARC. Yup, that's me . . . well, I'd better get going now.

TOUGH KID 1. Trying to get away, eh?

TOUGH KID 2. Getting away, eh?

MARC. Oh . . . no.

TOUGH KID 1. We can paint your face . . . with a black eye.

TOUGH KID 2. A black eye.

MARC. Don't you mean purple?

TOUGH KIDS 1 and 2. Huh?

MARC. An eye, if you hit it, turns purple. Not black, but purple.

(*A chase scene ensues. It has a slapstick quality.*)

MARC *thinks he got away and from behind him* TOUGH KID 1 *taps* MARC *on the shoulder.*)

TOUGH KID 1. Okay painter kid, we'll see if it turns black or purple. On the count of three. One . . . two . . . two and a half . . . two and five-eighths . . . (TOUGH KIDS 1 *and* 2 *start to exit but* MARC *does not see because he has his hands over his eyes.*) two and seven-eighths . . . two and ninety-nine one hundredths. (*They laugh.*)

(MARC *slowly uncovers his eyes and sees he is alone.*)

MARC. Don't come back or I'll give you a purple eye. (*He exits.*)

CHAGALL. Well, maybe I wasn't such a good fighter. Memories. Some of them you'd rather not remember. But in art class I could float away from others. In art class . . . in art class . . . I was king. In art class I was magic. In art class I was the only one who used a lot of purple. With my brush I made things come to life. I felt as if I was the brush. I touched the paint and I touched the paper and out of that came a cow that flew, a horse that rode on trails in the sky, and a giant that could take care of me and carry me on his shoulders over the town. All of these creatures I made into my very own circus. Yes, I made a whole circus, right in my painting.

MARC (*entering with circus drawing and* MOTHER). Look Mother, look at what I made for you.

MOTHER. Oh thank you, Marc. What is it?

MARC. What do you think? Do you like it?

MOTHER. Yes I do. You have talent.

MARC. Take it, Mother, please.

MOTHER. Thank you, Marc. Where did you get such talent?

MARC. I want to be a painter.

MOTHER. It might be better if you get a job as a clerk. It is good, steady work and they will pay you for it.

MARC. But I don't want to be a clerk, Mother. I want to make pictures.

MOTHER. Pictures? Hmm. I could get you a job working with a photographer. Yes . . . in a year you will get paid. Pictures are pictures.

MARC. Thank you, Mother. Taking pictures could be all right.

CHAGALL. Taking pictures could be all right.

MOTHER. Pictures are pictures.

(MOTHER *exits and whispers to* PHOTOGRAPHER *as she goes.* PHOTOGRAPHER *enters bringing a large portrait camera.*)

PHOTOGRAPHER. Yes? Could I help you?

MARC. I'm Marc Chagall.

PHOTOGRAPHER. Oh yes. Your mother told me.

MARC. I want to make pictures.

PHOTOGRAPHER. Yes, yes. I will make you an artist. This will be a real opportunity for you. In two years you may even be good enough to be paid.

MARC. I will be . . .

CHAGALL. . . . an artist.

PHOTOGRAPHER. Yes, but quiet. Here comes a customer. Hello, hello. Welcome to my studio.

(HUSBAND *and* WIFE *enter with four children.*)

HUSBAND. I want a picture of our family. A picture that will show all our true qualities. Can you do that?

PHOTOGRAPHER. Surely you jest. My pictures are so true to life that when your friends look at them, they will want to talk to them.

HUSBAND. It won't cost too much, will it?

PHOTOGRAPHER. No, no. Exactly the right amount.

HUSBAND. What do you think, dear?

WIFE. Well, I don't know, I . . . (*It seems as if she doesn't want to spend the money.*)

PHOTOGRAPHER. And who is this lovely lady?

HUSBAND. Oh . . . this is my wife.

PHOTOGRAPHER. I didn't know you were married to a beautiful model.

WIFE. I'm not really a . . .

PHOTOGRAPHER. Isn't she beautiful, Chagall?

MARC. Not really like a model, no.

PHOTOGRAPHER. Marc!

WIFE. We are so looking forward to seeing your pictures.

PHOTOGRAPHER. Yes, I'm looking forward to seeing them too.

CHAGALL. So you can get their money.

PHOTOGRAPHER. Stand there please, Marc.

(MARC *leads* HUSBAND, WIFE, *and children to position for the picture.*)

WIFE. Are you sure we look fine?

PHOTOGRAPHER. Wonderful, just wonderful. Now . . . big smiles. Look at the birdie. Ready, aim . . . (*They freeze with funny looks on their faces.*) How could they help but look wonderful? (*The family exits.*) Take this, Marc, and develop it. Oh, and Marc . . . you are a painter, aren't you?

MARC. Yes I am.

PHOTOGRAPHER. Well, they don't look as good as they think they do, so I'd like you to take your brush and touch them up a little.

MARC. But you said you took true to life pictures.

PHOTOGRAPHER. Never mind what I said! Just make them look pretty. (*He exits.*)

MARC. If that's what he wants, then that's what he'll get. Now let me see . . . a little bit here and a little bit there. I'll touch up her face, and I'll fill in his hair. I'll

make a line over here, and another line there. I'll push
in his nose, and fix up her hair.

(MARC *touches up the pictures and very funny faces
result.* PHOTOGRAPHER *enters.*)

PHOTOGRAPHER. Are you finished, Chagall?

CHAGALL. I certainly was.

PHOTOGRAPHER (*taking pictures from behind* MARC'S
back). Wha . . . What have you done to my picture?
You . . . you are . . . are

CHAGALL. Fired?

PHOTOGRAPHER. Fired! (*He takes the camera and leaves.*)

MARC. Fired. Oh . . . fired.

CHAGALL. Well, one career down the drain.

MOTHER (*entering with a blanket and making him lie
down on a bed which is another rostrum*). Forget
about it. Sleep tonight, and we'll talk about it in
the morning.

MARC. Yes, Mother.

(MOTHER *exits.*)

CHAGALL. I couldn't sleep that night . . . not after being
fired from my very first job.

MARC. I can't paint just like everyone else.

CHAGALL. Good for you.

MARC. Maybe I should only paint what my eyes see?

CHAGALL. What about what the heart feels . . . what
makes you laugh . . . what makes you cry . . . even
what scares you.

MARC. Nothing scares me.

CHAGALL. Oh? Nothing in a dark room? When you
are alone?

MARC. Alone? No, I'm not afraid.

CHAGALL. Of what's under your bed?

MARC. Under my bed?

CHAGALL. The creature that lives under your bed.

(**MARC** *is worried now. He wants to look, but . . . He hears a strange sound.*)

MARC. There is nothing under my bed.

CHAGALL. The creature that lives under your bed.

(*There is a sound and* **MARC** *sees the creature.*)

MARC. Ahh! (*He stands up on the bed, would like to leave but is afraid.*)

CHAGALL. Quick. Maybe you should run for the door.

MARC. No! He'll get my feet.

CHAGALL. On the count of three. One, two . . .

MARC. Two . . . oh what should I do?

MOTHER (*from off stage*). Marc? Are you having a dream?

MARC. Yes, Mother, I was only dreaming.

CHAGALL. Wouldn't you like to paint what is under your bed?

MARC. Don't be silly. There's nothing (*looking under*) under my bed.

CHAGALL. That's right. You just imagined it . . .

MARC. . . . in my head.

CHAGALL. Well? Wouldn't it be fun to paint what you imagined? Look around your room, Marc. What do you see?

MARC. It's only my room.

CHAGALL. Close your eyes. Remember? Your imagination?

MARC. It's my giant that carries me over the town. Or maybe an angel.

CHAGALL. Giants and angels. I remember once when I was alone, the roof blew apart, boards burst in all directions, lights . . .

MARC. . . . are pouring into my room, and an angel is flying down. It's beautiful.

(**MOTHER** *enters in time to hear the last part. She puts*

breakfast things on the rostrum to make it a table.
FATHER *enters and sits down at the table.*)

MOTHER. You certainly have an imagination, Marc.

CHAGALL. Imagination.

MARC. I can be a painter. Just let me take some classes with a painting teacher. I saw a sign that said a teacher gave painting lessons.

MOTHER. It won't be easy, Marc.

CHAGALL. Let me try.

MARC. I will work very hard.

MOTHER. We will see. What do you think, Father?

FATHER. It would be a waste of time and money. Who will pay a painter?

MOTHER. He could paint signs.

FATHER. Is that what you want to paint, Marc?

MARC. I want to be an artist.

MOTHER. Give him the money. Give him the lessons. He does have talent.

FATHER. If you want to paint . . . paint. Take my money. (FATHER *puts a small bag of money on the table and the parents exit.*)

CHAGALL. My parents loved me. They wanted what was best for me. I think I knew that even way back then.

MARC. I will be an artist, and lots of people will want to see and buy my work.
(PENNE, *the art teacher, enters with lumps of clay and a statue to copy. The statue and lumps of clay are actors in black body suits. They could be pulled in a wagon. The lump that* MARC *uses could be more than one actor.*)

PENNE. Ah, there you are. (*taking the money bag from* MARC). Welcome to Penne's School of Art. I will teach you everything there is to know about art. You can count on that.

MARC. I want to learn.

PENNE. Good. Well, just don't stand there. Take that lump of clay and do as I do.

MARC. Yes, sir.

PENNE. You must get the proportions correct.

(*The statue is set up and they are trying to copy it. PENNE is getting his lump more like the statue than is MARC. MARC has a very interesting shape and is even able to pull colored strands of material from his clay.*)

MARC. I'm trying.

PENNE. No, no, no. Your work must look like the real thing.

MARC. Like the real thing looks like on the outside, or on the inside?

PENNE. Uh . . . copy this statue.

MARC. Yes, sir.

PENNE. Now, I want the features, details, and the proportions.

CHAGALL. I tried to see as he did. But . . .

(**MARC** *pulls out a bunch of colors from the clay.*)

PENNE. Now, let's see your finished work.

CHAGALL. But it was not like him.

MARC. Here it is.

PENNE. Are you trying to be smart?

MARC. Yes, sir. I mean no, sir.

PENNE. This does not look like that.

CHAGALL. It does in a way.

PENNE. Don't be silly. Remember, if you do as I do and copy that statue, someday you will be just like me.

MARC. But I don't want to be just like you.

PENNE. Pardon?

CHAGALL. I said I don't want to paint the way you do.

PENNE. Preposterous! You will never be an artist then.

MARC. Yes I will.

PENNE. I can make a face that looks like a face.

MARC. I can made a face that shows what it is dreaming.

PENNE. I can make a person come true to life.

MARC. I can draw a man who will float over the town.

PENNE. I can draw the world as it is.

MARC. I can make my own world. I turn everything upside down and inside out. I can make the world dance. I can make the world sing . . .

PENNE. I can . . .

MARC. I can make a circus where there is nothing; I can paint love in all its colors.

PENNE. You are a fool. Now give up. You'll never be an artist. (PENNE'S *lump of clay and the statue to be copied leave.*) Get out and stay out. Never come back again! You are a failure. Your mother has wasted her money. Your dreams are nothing.

CHAGALL. I can make a circus in my head.

(MARC'S *sculpture exits with all its colors flying.* MARC *exits.*)

(*All the performers in the following circus scene are dressed in bright circus costumes. The one who is the ringmaster has a top hat and a megaphone. These are passed on to the next person when they become the ringmaster. There should be music with drums and trumpets, and the like.*)

RINGMASTER 1. Ladies and Gentlemen, I welcome you to the Circus Marc Chagall. All these brilliant acts are the finest, fanciest, funniest, most famous, most fantastic anywhere in the world. They are brought to you from us—thanks to that daring, dashing juggler of images, Marc Chagall.

(MARC *enters and juggles three brilliantly colored scarves. If he drops one, it could be picked up by* CHAGALL *who is always watching and sometimes participating invisibly with* MARC.)

RINGMASTER 2. Ladies and Gentlemen, let's give a big welcome for the next attraction under the Big Top . . .
The Georgi Family. They will perform one of the most difficult feats known in the circus, the full flip off the balance board.

(*The Georgi Family runs on and constructs a balance board with a plank and something to act as a fulcrum.*)

And now, let's give a really big hand for the star himself, the one, the only, the magnificent, Petrov Georgi . . . Here he is!

(*Petrov Georgi enters. He is a life-sized rag doll that can be made to do anything. He is manipulated as a kind of large puppet.*)

Silence please, Ladies and Gentlemen. And now the dangerous full flip off the balance board . . . Maestro a drum roll!

(*When the drum roll ends, one of the family jumps with a yell on one end of the balance board and, with the help of the other family members, Petrov Georgi does a flip and takes a bow.*)

RINGMASTER 3. Ladies and Gentlemen, Mr. Marc Chagall, at great expense, has brought the largest trio of trained pachyderms, that means elephants to you, to be found in all Russia. All eyes on the centre ring.

(MARC *enters as an animal trainer and gets the elephants [who are people] to do circus tricks. They perform a parade of holding one another's tails with their trunks. They even perform a dance. They could also show the courage of* MARC *by letting them stand on him. They exit, and* MARC *bows and exits.*)

RINGMASTER 4. Ladies and Gentlemen, walk on the edge and float over your heads. You take a lady, add an umbrella, and you have an angel . . . on a tightrope.

(*A girl performs the act on the ground. She shows the danger of walking on a tightrope by wobbling. The crowd and* RINGMASTER *respond with "oohs" and "ahhs."*)

RINGMASTER 5. Ladies and Gentlemen, for our final act we have a man who will be shot from the mouth of a cannon. Yes, a man who will be shot from the mouth of this very cannon. He will be propelled through the air and land in the safety of our newly repaired net.

(*A silk net is brought out which has an obvious patch. It is controlled by two people.*)

The net! And here to perform this act is our very own star—Petrov Georgi!

(*The rag doll Petrov Georgi enters and is bowing during the next speech.*)

Ladies and Gentlemen, you will see for the first time and maybe the last time this dangerous, dreaded, death-defying dive . . .

(*Petrov Georgi looks like he has second thoughts.*)

The great Petrov will be shot from this cannon (*a hollow tube*) and land in this net . . . we hope.

(*Petrov Georgi is being forced into the cannon.*)

Maestro, a drum roll please.

(*A drum roll sounds across the stage.*)

The fuse . . . the match.

(*The sound of the drum is followed by a big bang. Petrov Georgi flies in a looping way, turned and twisted by the actors, toward the net. The net is moving all over the place and, of course, misses him.*)

The ambulance!

(*The ambulance siren sounds and there is a flashing light. The light could be as simple as the opening and closing of hands. Petrov is loaded on to the ambulance and . . .*)

To the hospital!

(*The circus exits to the hospital amidst much bowing and excitement.* MARC *enters as the circus exits.*)

MOTHER (*bringing back on the circus painting*). You did not do well in art school. You cannot be a painter, my son.

MARC. There are other schools. But I did learn something.

MOTHER. Don't worry, you can always get a real job . . . remember? A clerk.

CHAGALL. What are you doing?

(MOTHER *is taking the circus painting and putting it on the floor to be a rug.*)

MARC. My painting!

MOTHER. Yes, it's a good thick cloth. It makes a beautiful rug.

MARC. It was my painting.

CHAGALL. She just didn't understand.

MOTHER. I'm sorry, Marc.

(MOTHER *exits and* MARC *picks up the painting that has been walked on.*)

MARC. Maybe you are right. I can be a clerk.

CHAGALL. I still wanted to be a painter; but could I find my dream again?

(BELLA *enters. She is a smiling woman.*)

BELLA. Could I see what you're holding?

CHAGALL. Her name is Bella. An angel who walked.

BELLA. May I see it, please?

MARC. Why? Do you want to wipe your feet?

BELLA. What?

MARC. Oh . . . nothing.

BELLA. I'd just like to look at it.

CHAGALL. Will she laugh at my paintings?

(BELLA *laughs.*)

MARC. You think it's stupid, don't you?

BELLA. No. Your painting laughs, so I want to laugh too.

MARC. You mean you like it?

BELLA. Yes.

CHAGALL. She liked it!

BELLA. I wish I could have one just like it in my room.

MARC. I can fill your room with paintings. I can put you in my paintings . . . May I put you in my paintings?

CHAGALL. I thought I could paint her into my life. If she were in my pictures, I thought she would always be near. I'd help make her wings.

BELLA. You want to paint me?

MARC. Can you fly?

BELLA. If you show me.

CHAGALL. She didn't laugh. She knew what I meant. She was my angel. I could see her, touch her; I could soar with her. After we had taken some time together, I wanted to ask her to marry me.

(*While* CHAGALL *is talking,* MARC *and* BELLA *walk and talk with a lot of gestures. They sit together and . . .*)

MARC. Bella, would you . . .

BELLA. Would I what?

MARC. Would you . . . be interested . . .

CHAGALL. Go ahead. Ask her if she would marry you.

MARC. Will you . . .

BELLA. Will you marry me?

MARC. What? Yes! Sure! Mazel Tov!

(MARC *and* BELLA *exit to get ready for the wedding.*)

CHAGALL. Everyone has wedding pictures. I remember my wedding like a picture; well, more like a comic book. If Bella had asked me to paint a picture of our wedding, this is how I would have painted it. There would be relatives, and friends of relatives. You could see them talk. (*The following scene can be done with puppets or actors. If actors are used, they should use masks.*

Balloons with painted faces can also be used, including many different kinds of puppets.)

GUEST. When is Marc Chagall going to get here?

RELATIVE. The sooner the wedding is over, the sooner we can all eat.

DISTANT COUSIN. No, worse. Pictures. He says he's an artist.

GUEST. Yes, but what does he do for a living?

DISTANT COUSIN. That's just it! Nothing! He just paints.

RELATIVE. Poor Bella.

ALL. Tsk, tsk, tsk.

CHAGALL. Talk, talk, talk. Sometimes all that talk reminded me of so many geese. But now, there we are, coming down the centre of my wedding picture. And who comes along but my mother and father, holding me so I don't float away. There would be another picture of me . . . waiting under the Hupah. (MARC *enters as described. The Hupah is the tent-like covering used in Jewish weddings.*)

HUPAH HOLDER. Here she comes.

CHAGALL. I remember she looked truly like an angel. (*The wedding music starts.*) I was frozen, as if my blood had stopped moving. If I smiled, my face would have cracked. The ceremony began. The Rabbi . . .

RABBI. Blessed be he that cometh in the name of the Lord, we have blessed you out of the house of the Lord.

CHAGALL. Ceremony, solemnity, and ritual mixed with a gaggle of relatives.

MARC. Behold, you are consecrated to me with this ring as my wife, according to the law of Moses and Israel.

CHAGALL. We looked inside of each other. We spoke without words.

RABBI. Soon may be heard in the cities of Judah . . .

RABBI, HUPAH HOLDER. . . . and the streets of Jerusalem . . .

Rabbi, Hupah Holder, Chagall. . . . the voice of joy and gladness . . .

Rabbi, Hupah Holder, Chagall, Marc. . . . the voice of the Bridegroom . . .

Rabbi, Hupah Holder, Chagall, Marc, Bella. . . . and the voice of the Bride.

All. Mazel Tov!

Chagall. Ahh! And now the wedding dance begins, and all the guests join in, if not by dancing at least by clapping.

(*The entire cast joins in. The dancers gradually spin away leaving only* **Marc** *and* **Bella.**)

We went to the countryside for our honeymoon, to a place beside a field of cows. It was more like a milk-moon . . . cows, horses, Bella and I both flew over the moon.

(**Bella** *dances as she exits off-stage.*)

Too soon the war broke out, and Mother finally got her wish. I became a clerk in the army.

(*A sound collage of war sounds, a soldier with a gun runs by and gives* **Marc** *an army hat, coat, rifle, pen, and paper.*)

Soldiers shooting, people fleeing, hurting, bleeding, dying. No food, fathers killed, children hungry. Anger festered all around. Tears washed the faces and fields of war.

(**Accusers 1, 2, 3,** *and* **4** *run from opposite sides of the stage and yell to one another in a relay of blame.*)

Accuser 1. The generals are to blame.

Accuser 2. No, it's the German's fault.

Accuser 3. It's the Czar's fault.

Accuser 4. It's their fault.

Accusers (*to* **Marc**). It's the Jews' fault.

(*They exit.*)

CHAGALL. My people are blamed, and fled as of old.

MARC (*starting to draw on the paper he has on a clipboard*). I want to paint my people into my pictures so they will be safe. I will make places in my pictures where they can hide.

(RUSSIAN OFFICIAL, *dressed as pompously as possible, enters.*)

RUSSIAN OFFICIAL. Mr. Chagall? Mr. Marc Chagall? Oh, there you are. Mr. Chagall, we have a job from the government for you.

MARC. Oh? What kind of a job?

RUSSIAN OFFICIAL. We would like you to be the art supervisor for your home town of Vitebsk.

MARC. Me? What could I do?

RUSSIAN OFFICIAL. You can make the town come alive with art of the people.

MARC. Well, that would be great!

CHAGALL. I thought I could make the whole town as magical as one of my paintings.

MARC. All you painters of Vitebsk! We are going to make this town fly.

CHAGALL. Most of them were the painters of the beautiful little signs that hung above the shops.

MARC. Get all your colors and we'll paint horses and cows and roosters and whatever we dream, all over the walls and roofs of our town. (*to the audience*) Now get all your colors.

CHAGALL. I brought my favorite colors, even good old purple.

RUSSIAN OFFICIAL. All we really want is some statues of the politicians.

MARC. Yes. (*not really listening to the* RUSSIAN OFFICIAL) And we can have a school for all the artists in the community; a place where children can find a love of art.

We can make giant kites and fly colors to the sky . . .

RUSSIAN OFFICIAL. Just a minute . . .

MARC. Every home shall be a gallery of art, and every
person an artist.

RUSSIAN OFFICIAL. Stop!

MARC. What's the matter?

RUSSIAN OFFICIAL. You are going too far.

MARC. What do you mean? I'm doing what you asked.
I am making the town come alive with the art of
its people.

RUSSIAN OFFICIAL. That's all very well; but you see, all we
really need is some statues of the political leaders to
go in the park.

MARC. That's all you want?

RUSSIAN OFFICIAL. That, and no more!

(*The* RUSSIAN OFFICIAL *exits.*)

CHAGALL. He wanted so little. He turned my colors black.
He was the kind who doesn't like stars because they
don't line up in neat rows. Bella had warned me. But
I still couldn't find my colors.

MARC. I don't want to paint anymore.

BELLA (*entering*). Let your colors, your dreams, your
heart, and your laugh—let them fly away in your
paintings.

MARC. But . . .

BELLA. Let me feel your colors.

(*She starts to exit.*)

MARC. I've run out of colors.

BELLA. Feel all your colors.

(*She is gone.* MARC *exits after her. There is a pause.*)

CHAGALL. I can't stay sad forever. Circus clowns start
bumping into my gloom, and stars follow me to
work. I can paint anything. I see with more than my
eyes. I see how I will paint you and even you! I need

lots of purple for you. A dollop of red, a touch of green, maybe you have stripes and dots. Your feet don't touch the ground. Watch the roof! You're going to fly higher than my cows. You save a small space in your pictures for me to sneak into . . . and I will save a place for you in mine.

On Being Female, Black, and Free

From the essay "On Being Female, Black, and Free"
by Margaret Walker

Ever since I was a little girl I have wanted to write and I have been writing. My father told my mother it was only a puberty urge and would not last, but he encouraged my early attempts at rhyming verses just the same, and he gave me the notebook or daybook in which to keep my poems together. When I was eighteen and had ended my junior year in college, my father laughingly agreed it was probably more than a puberty urge. I had filled the 365 pages with poems.

Writing has always been a means of expression for me and for other black Americans who are just like me, who feel, too, the need for freedom in this "home of the brave, and land of the free." From the first, writing meant learning the craft and developing the art. Going to school had one major goal, to learn to be a writer. As early as my eighth year I had the desire, at ten I was trying, at eleven and twelve I was learning, and at fourteen and fifteen I was seeing my first things printed in local school and community papers. I have a copy of a poem published in 1930 and an article with the caption, "What Is to Become of Us?" which appeared in 1931 or 1932. All of this happened before I went to Northwestern.

I spent fifteen years becoming a poet before my first book appeared in 1942. I was learning my craft, finding my voice, seeking discipline as life imposes and superimposes that discipline upon the artist. Perhaps my home environment was most important in the early stages—hearing my mother's music, my sister and brother playing the piano, reading my father's books, hearing his sermons, and trying every day to write a poem. Meanwhile, I found I would have to start all over again and learn how to write prose fiction in order to write the novel I was determined to create to the best of my ability and thus fulfill my promise to my grandmother. A novel is not written exactly the same way as a poem, especially a long novel and a short poem. The creative process may be basically the same—that is, the thinking or conceptualization—but the techniques, elements, and form or craft are decidedly and distinctively different.

It has always been my feeling that writing must come out of living, and the writer is no more than his personality endures in the crucible of his times. As a woman, I have come through the fires of hell because I am a black woman, because I am poor, because I live in America, and because I am determined to be both a creative artist and maintain my inner integrity and my instinctive need to be free.

I don't think I noticed the extreme discrimination against women while I was growing up in the South. The economic struggle to exist and the racial dilemma occupied all my thinking until I was more than an adult woman. My mother had undergone all kinds of discrimination in academia because of her sex; so have my sisters. Only after I went back to school and earned a doctorate did I begin to notice discrimination against me as a woman. It seems the higher you try to climb, the more rarefied the air, the more obstacles appear. I realize I had been naïve, that the issues had not been obvious and that as early as my first employment I felt the sting of discrimination because I am female. . . .

Despite severe illness and painful poverty, and despite jobs that always discriminated against me as a woman— never paying me equal money for equal work, always threatening or replacing me with a man or men who were neither as well educated nor experienced but just men— despite all these examples of discrimination I have managed to work toward being a self-fulfilling, re-creating, reproducing woman, raising a family, writing poetry, cooking food, doing all the creative things I know how to do and enjoy. But my problems have not been simple; they have been manifold. Being female, black, and poor in America means I was born with three strikes against me. I am considered at the bottom of the social class-caste system in these United States, born low on the totem pole. If "a black man has no rights that a white man is bound to respect," what about a black woman? . . .

A writer needs certain conditions in which to work and create art. She needs a piece of time; a peace of mind; a quiet place; and a private life.

Early in my life I discovered I had to earn my living and I would not be able to eke out the barest existence as a writer. Nobody writes while hungry, sick, tired, and worried. Maybe you can manage with one of these but not all four at one time. Keeping the wolf from the door has been my full-time job for more than forty years.

Thirty-six of those years I have spent in the college classroom, and nobody writes to full capacity on a full-time teaching job. My life has been public, active, and busy to the point of constant turmoil, tumult, and trauma. Sometimes the only quiet and private place where I could write a sonnet was in the bathroom, because that was the only room where the door could be locked and no one would intrude. I have written mostly at night in my adult life and especially since I have been married, because I was determined not to neglect any members of my family; so I cooked every meal daily, washed dishes and dirty clothes, and nursed sick babies.

The **Pot** Child

A short story by Jane Yolen

There was once an ill-humored potter who lived all alone and made his way by shaping clay into cups and bowls and urns. His pots were colored with the tones of the earth, and on their sides he painted all creatures excepting man.

"For there was never a human I liked well enough to share my house and my life with," said the bitter old man.

But one day, when the potter was known throughout the land for his sharp tongue as well as his pots, and so old that even death might have come as a friend, he sat down and on the side of a large bisque urn he drew a child.

The child was without flaw in the outline, and so the potter colored in its form with earth glazes: rutile for the body and cobalt blue for the eyes. And to the potter's practiced eye, the figure on the pot was perfect.

So he put the pot into the kiln, closed up the door with bricks, and set the flame.

Slowly the fires burned. And within the kiln the glazes matured and turned their proper tones.

It was a full day and a night before the firing was done. And a full day and a night before the kiln had cooled. And it was a full day and a night before the old potter dared unbrick the kiln door. For the pot child was his masterpiece, of this he was sure.

At last, though, he could put it off no longer. He took down the kiln door, reached in, and removed the urn.

Slowly he felt along the pot's side. It was smooth and still warm. He set the pot on the ground and walked around it, nodding his head as he went.

The child on the pot was so lifelike, it seemed to follow him with its lapis eyes. Its skin was a pearly yellow-white, and each hair on its head like beaten gold.

So the old potter squatted down before the urn, examining the figure closely, checking it for cracks and flaws, but there were none. He drew in his breath at the child's beauty and thought to himself, "*There* is one I might like well enough." And when he expelled his breath again, he blew directly on the image's lips.

At that, the pot child sighed and stepped off the urn.

Well, this so startled the old man, that he fell back into the dust.

After a while, though, the potter saw that the pot child was waiting for him to speak. So he stood up and in a brusque tone said "Well, then, come here. Let me look at you."

The child ran over to him and, ignoring his tone, put its arms around his waist, and whispered "Father" in a high sweet voice.

This so startled the old man that he was speechless for the first time in his life. And as he could not find the words to tell the child to go, it stayed. Yet after a day, when he had found the words, the potter knew he could not utter them for the child's perfect face and figure had enchanted him.

When the potter worked or ate or slept, the child was by his side, speaking when spoken to but otherwise still. It was a pot child, after all, and not a real child. It did not join him in his work but was content to watch. When other people came to the old man's shop, the child stepped back onto the urn and did not move. Only the potter knew it was alive.

One day several famous people came to the potter's shop. He showed them all around, grudgingly, touching one pot and then another. He answered their questions in a voice that was crusty and hard. But they knew his reputation and did not answer back.

At last they came to the urn.

The old man stood before it and sighed. It was such an uncharacteristic sound that the people looked at him strangely. But the potter did not notice. He simply stood for a moment more, then said, "This is the Pot Child. It is my masterpiece. I shall never make another one so fine."

He moved away, and one woman said after him. "It *is* good." But turning to her companions, she added in a low voice, "But it is *too* perfect for me."

A man with her agreed. "It lacks something," he whispered back.

The woman thought a moment. "It has no heart," she said. "That is what is wrong."

"It has no soul," he amended.

They nodded at each other and turned away from the urn. The woman picked out several small bowls, and, paying for them, she and the others went away.

No sooner were the people out of sight than the pot child stepped down from the urn.

"Father," the pot child asked, "what is a heart?"

"A vastly overrated part of the body," said the old man gruffly. He turned to work the clay on his wheel.

"Then," thought the pot child, "I am better off without one." It watched as the clay grew first tall and then wide between the potter's knowing palms. It hesitated asking another question, but at last could bear it no longer.

"And what is a soul, Father?" asked the pot child. "Why did you not draw one on me when you made me on the urn?"

The potter looked up in surprise. "Draw one? No one can draw a soul."

The child's disappointment was so profound, the potter added, "A man's body is like a pot, which does not disclose what is inside. Only when the pot is poured, do we see its contents. Only when a man acts, do we know what kind of soul he has."

The pot child seemed happy with that explanation, and the potter went back to his work. But over the next few weeks the child continually got in his way. When the potter worked the clay, the pot child tried to bring him water to keep the clay moist. But it spilled the water and the potter pushed the child away.

When the potter carried the unfired pots to the kiln, the pot child tried to carry some, too. But it dropped the pots, and many were shattered. The potter started to cry out in anger, bit his tongue, and was still.

When the potter went to fire the kiln, the pot child tried to light the flame. Instead, it blew out the fire.

At last the potter cried, "You heartless thing. Leave me to do my work. It is all I have. How am I to keep body and soul together when I am so plagued by you?"

At these words, the pot child sat down in the dirt,

covered its face, and wept. Its tiny body heaved so with its sobs that the potter feared it would break in two. His crusty old heart softened, and he went over to the pot child and said, "There, child. I did not mean to shout so. What is it that ails you?"

The pot child looked up. "Oh, my Father, I know I have no heart. But that is a vastly overrated part of the body. Still, I was trying to show how I was growing a soul."

The old man looked startled for a minute, but then, recalling their conversation of many weeks before, he said "My poor pot child, no one can *grow* a soul. It is there from birth." He touched the child lightly on the head.

The potter had meant to console the child, but at that the child cried even harder than before. Drops sprang from its eyes and ran down its cheeks like blue glaze. "Then I shall never have a soul," the pot child cried. "For I was not born but made."

Seeing how the child suffered, the old man took a deep breath. And when he let it out again, he said, "Child, as I made you, now I will make you a promise. When I die, you shall have *my* soul for then I shall no longer need it."

"Oh, then I will be truly happy," said the pot child, slipping its little hand gratefully into the old man's. It did not see the look of pain that crossed the old man's face. But when it looked up at him and smiled, the old man could not help but smile back.

That very night, under the watchful eyes of the pot child, the potter wrote out his will. It was a simple paper, but it took a long time to compose for words did not come easily to the old man. Yet as he wrote, he felt surprisingly lightened. And the pot child smiled at him all the while. At last, after many scratchings out, it was done. The potter read the paper aloud to the pot child.

"It is good," said the pot child. "You do not suppose I will have long to wait for my soul?"

The old man laughed. "Not long, child."

And then the old man slept, tired after the late night's labor. But he had been so busy writing, he had forgotten to bank his fire, and in the darkest part of the night, the flames went out.

In the morning the shop was ice cold, and so was the old man. He did not waken, and without him, the pot child could not move from its shelf.

Later in the day, when the first customers arrived, they found the old man. And beneath his cold fingers lay a piece of paper that said:

> When I am dead, place my body in
> my kiln and light the flames. And
> when I am nothing but ashes, let
> those ashes be placed inside the
> Pot Child. For I would be one, body
> and soul, with the earth I have worked.

So it was done as the potter wished. And when the kiln was opened up, the people of the town placed the ashes in the ice-cold urn.

At the touch of the hot ashes, the pot cracked: once across the breast of the child and two small fissures under its eyes.

"What a shame," said the people to one another on seeing that. "We should have waited until the ashes cooled."

Yet the pot was still so beautiful, and the old potter so well known, that the urn was placed at once in a museum. Many people came to gaze on it.

One of those was the woman who had seen the pot that day so long ago at the shop.

"Why, look," she said to her companions. "It is the pot the old man called his masterpiece. It *is* good. But I like it even better now with those small cracks."

"Yes," said one of her companions, "it was too perfect before."

"Now the pot child has real character," said the woman. "It has . . . heart."

"Yes," added the same companion, "it has soul."

And they spoke so loudly that all the people around them heard. The story of their conversation was printed and repeated throughout the land, and everyone who went by the pot stopped and murmured, as if part of a ritual, "Look at that pot child. It has such heart. It has such soul."

"Ah," sighed the Dream Weaver when the tale was done. It was a great relief to her to have it over, both the weaving and the telling. She dropped her hands to her sides and thought about the artist of the tale and how he alone really knew when his great work was done, and how he had put his own heart and soul into it. For what was art, she thought, but the heart and soul made visible.

"I thank you, my young friends," she said to the boy and girl as they waited, hand upon hand, until she was through. "And now I can go home and sleep."

She finished the piece of weaving and held it up to them. "Will you take this one with you?" she asked.

"But it was your dream," said the boy hesitantly.

The girl was more honest still. "There is nothing on it, Dream Weaver. On that—or on the other."

"Nothing? What do you mean—nothing?" Her voice trembled.

"A jumble of threads," said the girl. "Tightly woven, true, but with no picture or pattern."

"No picture? Nothing visible? Was there never a picture?" asked the old woman, her voice low.

"While you told the tale," said the boy, "there were pictures aplenty in my head and in my heart."

"And on the cloth?"

"I do not really know," admitted the girl. "For your voice spun the tale so well, I scarcely knew anything more."

"Ah," said the Dream Weaver. She was silent for a moment and then said, more to herself than to the two, "So that is why no one takes their dreams."

"We will take your weaving if it would please you," said the boy.

The Dream Weaver put away her loom and threads. "It does not matter," she said. "I see that now. Memory is the daughter of the ear and the eye. I know you will take the dream with you, in your memory, and it will last long past the weaving."

They helped her strap the baskets to her back. "Long past," they assured her. Then they watched as the Dream Weaver threaded her way down the crooked streets to her home.

The Haste-Me-Well Quilt

A short story by Elizabeth Yates

Simon lay very still in his bed. Outside, birds were singing in the apple tree; cows were mooing by the pasture bars as they did when it was time to be milked.

Sometimes the wind flapped a little at the drawn shade, lifting it and letting in a flash of sunshine to frolic through the darkened room. But Simon only turned restlessly on the bed, kicking at the sheet and sending his books and toys onto the floor. He was tired of lying still, tired of being sick. He was cross at the world.

A set of crayons that his father had brought him that morning toppled off the bed. The blue one lay broken. Simon was glad it was broken and wished they all were. He did not want to use them. He hated crayons. He hated everyone. He—

Then the door opened slowly. It was Grandmother, with something over her arm. She went quietly across to the window, raising the shade so the sunlight could come into the room. The scent of lilacs came, too, and the song of birds.

Simon screwed up his eyes and said crossly, "Don't want any light, want darkness."

Grandmother laid the quilt she was carrying across the end of his bed; then she sat down on the bed and took one of Simon's hands in hers. She put her other hand on his forehead. Her touch was cool and gentle, like the water of a brook on a summer day. Simon opened his eyes and stared at her.

"'Truly the light is sweet, and a pleasant thing it is for the eyes to behold the sun,'" Grandmother said slowly. "That's in the Bible, Simon. Grandfather read it to me this morning before he went out to plant the corn."

Simon opened his eyes wider. Grandmother had put something at the end of his bed. It was a patchwork quilt. Simon looked at it curiously. It was made not of odd-shaped patterns sewn together, but of tiny pictures of real things.

"Granny, what have you got?" he asked, forgetting how cross he was at the world, forgetting his hot, heavy head.

"This, Simon, is a quilt that we have always laid on the bed of sickness. Because of that it is called the Haste-Me-Well Quilt."

Deftly she shook it out of its folds and spread it over Simon, saying as she did so, "Grandfather needs you to help him on the farm. Your father wants to take a strong boy back to the city with him. It's time that you got well."

"Is it a magic quilt?" Simon asked, fingering it warily.

Grandmother nodded. "Perhaps, but a very special kind of magic."

Then something happened to Simon. He smiled. And because he had not smiled for a week but only thought how sorry he was for himself, his lips were a little stiff at the corners. But the smile lived on in his eyes, dark and deep, almost as dark as his thick black hair.

"Tell me about it, please," he said, snuggling down under the quilt and pulling Grandmother's hand up to his chin.

"Long ago, Simon," she began, "more than a hundred years ago, my grandmother—"

"*Your* grandmother!" he exclaimed—such a long way that seemed to reach back into the past.

"Yes," Grandmother nodded, "Lucy, her name was, made the quilt. She lived on a farm on the moors close to the Scottish border. She was not much older than you when she started it, and she finished it when she was seventeen—in time for her marriage. All of her friends were making quilts, but they made them out of bits and pieces of calico cut into squares or circles or triangles and sewed together into pretty patterns. Lucy was gay and strong, with quick fingers and a lively mind. She wanted to do something different, so she cut out her bits of calico into little pictures."

Grandmother bent over the quilt, and Simon propped his head up to follow her finger's journey across it.

"See, here is the farmhouse where she lived on the edge of the moors. Here are the chickens and the old tabby. Here is the postman, the muffin man with his bell, and the peddler who came with trinkets and ribbons and pots and pans. Here is her father, going off with his crook for the sheep. Here is a teakettle and the footstool at her feet, tables and fire tongs, watering cans and a bellows, horses and snails, a great castle, and a coach with dashing horses. Things she read about in books are here, like dragons and kangaroos and gladiators, as well as the latest fashion in bonnets and a mirror to try them on before"— Grandmother got more and more excited as her fingers flew across the quilt and she pointed out its wonders.

"It *is* a magic quilt," Simon agreed.

"Whatever young Lucy saw as interesting, useful, or amusing," Grandmother went on, "she snipped out of calico and sewed onto a white square, which was sewed to all the other white squares. Then, see, Simon, around the border she planted an old-fashioned garden!"

"It's like your garden, Granny, here at Easterly Farm!" Simon exclaimed.

"That's because it was *her* garden," Grandmother said quietly.

"It was?"

"Yes. When Lucy married, she and her husband came to America, here to this New England countryside. It was close to wilderness then, you must remember, but with their own hands they built this house; and while Silas cleared the fields and planted his crops and raised his stock, Lucy brought up her family—five boys and five girls, each one with a name from the Bible."

"And the quilt?"

"It must have meant everything to her in those days, for it was all her past—beautiful and orderly and gracious—and she brought it forward into a life of hardship and toil and privation. To her it was the tale of an age that was gone forever, costumes and customs, the little things used in a house and the larger things that though never seen were talked about; and she made it the background of a new life."

"How did it get its name, Granny? You haven't told me that."

Grandmother smiled. "The quilt used to lie on the guest bed, for all to admire it and for its occasional use. Then one day Peter was sick. He was the eldest of the five boys. He was wracked with chills and nothing they could do seemed to warm him. Lucy put all the blankets she had over him, and finally the quilt. Soon, oh, much sooner than anyone thought possible, the chills shivered themselves away and he went to sleep. Ever after that the quilt was put on the bed of a child who was sick."

"Was it ever on my father's bed?" Simon asked.

"Yes." Grandmother looked away. "Once when he fell from the barn during the haying and hurt his back, the doctor said that he could not do anything for him because he could not keep him still long enough." Grandmother smiled and turned back to look at Simon. "Grandfather and I didn't give up so easily. We put the quilt on his bed and for days and days afterward your father had wonderful adventures with it. He was always going to tell me about them, but he always forgot to."

Simon was looking drowsy, so Grandmother smoothed the folds of the quilt as it lay over him and stole softly from the room.

Simon moved his fingers lovingly over the quilt. He stroked the furry rabbit and called to the horse galloping across the field. He waved to the coach as it dashed along the road to London, and he bought a muffin from the muffin man. Then he opened the gate in the white fence that enclosed the farmhouse from the rolling moors and went up to the wide front door. Seeing it from a distance, he had not thought he could possibly go through the door, but the nearer he got to it the more of a size they were, and he found himself going into the house.

Inside, it was cool and quiet. His steps echoed a bit on the polished brick of the floor, but the sound did not disturb the tabby sleeping by the hearth. On the hob hung a fat kettle with a wisp of steam coming from its spout, saying as clearly as any words that whoever might be passing would be welcome to a dish of tea.

Simon went to the end of a passage and pushed open another door. A young girl was sitting by an open window. Grandmother had not told him what Lucy looked like, but Simon knew right away that this was Lucy. The quilt lay in a heap on the floor beside her; on a table nearby were scissors and thread, and bits and pieces of cloth. Simon crossed the room and stood beside Lucy. She looked up at him.

"I have a little boy in the quilt," she said. "There's no room for you."

"That's all right," Simon replied, "but mayn't I sit down and watch you?"

"If you wish," she smiled, "but it's all finished."

Simon sat down, tailor fashion before her, cupping his chin in his hands.

"Two hundred and seventy-four squares around a center panel, bordered by flowers," Lucy went on. "It's all done, but it's well it is for I'm going away next week."

"Where are you going?" Simon asked.

"To the New World." Lucy looked out of the window and Simon thought her voice throbbed, like a bird's on a low note. "I shall never see England again, never the rolling moors, nor the mountains of Scotland."

"*Never?*" Simon echoed. What a long time that was.

She shook her head slowly. "Ever since I was a little girl I have been cutting out and patching together the things that are my world. Now I can take my old world with me into the new. Once I wished I could draw pictures, go to London, and study to be an artist, but—"

"Why didn't you?" Simon demanded.

"If I had been a man I should have, but a girl doesn't do those things. Scissors, thread, thimble, calico—those are my artist's tools. Fingers are wonderful things, aren't they, little boy? You put a tool in them—it doesn't matter what it is—a hoe, a churn, a needle, a spoon—and they do the rest."

"My father gave me crayons to draw with," Simon confided. "I want to be an artist someday."

"Crayons?" Lucy looked as if the word were strange to her. "They'll not make you an artist, but fingers will."

"Why?"

"Because they are friends to all you're feeling. I didn't know when I started this quilt that it would mean so much to me. Now, though I'm going far away, everything I love is going with me."

Simon stroked the quilt. "It will be nice to have it on your bed, won't it?"

She laughed. "Oh, it won't ever be on my bed. It's too good for that! It'll be in the spare room, for guests to use when they come to stay with us."

"And it will be on the children's beds whenever they are sick," Simon went on.

Lucy looked at him, amazed. "What a strange idea!"

"It will make them well."

"Do you really think so, little boy?" Lucy looked incredulous, then her eyes gazed far away as if she did not see Simon at all and she said slowly, "The quilt could never do that, but perhaps the thoughts I have sewed into it could." Her eyes came back from the faraway place and she looked closely at Simon. "What is your name, little boy? I would like to know in case we meet again."

"Simon."

She wrinkled her brows. "Yes, Simon. For a moment I thought you were one of my boys." She went on looking at him as if wondering why he seemed so familiar, then she shook her head.

"There's magic in the quilt," Simon commented, reaching out and touching it.

"Magic? What strange words you use."

"But there is," Simon insisted. "How did you put it in?"

She laughed gaily. "What you call magic is just being happy in what you are doing, loving it the way you love the morning or the new lambs every spring. There's strength in happiness."

The blind was flapping at the window. The scent of lilacs filled the air. The sun, dropping low over the hills, was coming into the room like an arrow of gold. Simon drew his hands over the quilt and propped himself up on his elbows. On the floor lay his crayons, one of them broken.

He slipped out of bed and gathered the crayons together into their box, then he pushed the pillows up straight and climbed back into bed. Leaning against the pillows, he curved his knees up so his drawing pad might rest against them. He was sad that the blue crayon was broken, for so much blue was needed to arch the sky over the rolling moors and give life to Lucy's eyes. But he would manage somehow.

Quickly he worked, his fingers strong and free, eager with happiness, hurrying to do something for Grandmother that he might have a present for her when she came back to his room.

The door pushed open a little, then wider as Grandmother saw Simon. On the table by his bed she laid a small tray.

"There's a glass of milk from the afternoon's milking, Simon," she said. "Grandfather sent it up to you, and I thought you'd like a molasses cookie from a batch I've just made."

Simon finished his picture quickly.

"See, Granny, I have a present for you!"

Grandmother smiled as she took the drawing. It was a happy picture; well-done, too. Simon's father would be pleased with it. A young girl and a patchwork quilt, and in the background a small stone farmhouse. Grandmother looked closer. It was the Haste-Me-Well Quilt and Lucy looking at the world with eyes of wonder.

"Thank you, Simon, thank you very much, but I did not tell you my grandmother's eyes were blue, did I?"

Simon shook his head. "Were they?"

"Yes, blue as morning light on the mountains, and her fingers were fine and strong."

Fingers were wonderful things, Simon thought. It didn't much matter what they held if they held it with joy. Simon looked dreamily across the room. He was trying to remember something to tell Grandmother, but whatever it was it was slipping from him like a rainbow before full sunshine.

"May I get up now, Granny, please?" he asked.

A surprised smile lighted Grandmother's face. She nodded and began to fold up the Haste-Me-Well Quilt.

THE **BRIDGE** BUILDER

A short story by Margaret Mahy

My father was a bridge builder. That was his business
—crossing chasms, joining one side of the river with the
other.

When I was small, bridges brought us bread and
books, Christmas crackers and coloured pencils—one-
span bridges over creeks, two-span bridges over streams,
three-span bridges over wide rivers. Bridges sprang from
my father's dreams threading roads together—girder
bridges, arched bridges, suspension bridges, bridges of
wood, bridges of iron or concrete. Like a sort of hero, my
father would drive piles and piers through sand and mud
to the rocky bones of the world. His bridges became visible parts of the world's hidden skeleton. When we went
out on picnics it was along roads held together by my
father's works. As we crossed rivers and ravines we heard
each bridge singing in its own private language. We could

hear the melody, but my father was the only one who understood the words.

There were three of us when I was small: Philippa, the oldest, Simon in the middle, and me, Merlin, the youngest, the one with the magician's name. We played where bridges were being born, running around piles of sand and shingle, bags of cement and bars of reinforced steel. Concrete mixers would turn, winches would wind, piles would be driven and decking cast. Slowly, as we watched and played, a bridge would appear and people could cross over.

For years my father built bridges where people said they wanted them, while his children stretched up and out in three different directions. Philippa became a doctor and Simon an electrical engineer, but I became a traveller, following the roads of the world and crossing the world's bridges as I came to them.

My father, however, remained a bridge builder. When my mother died and we children were grown up and gone, and there was no more need for balloons and books or Christmas crackers and coloured pencils, his stored powers were set free and he began to build the bridges he saw in his dreams.

The first of his new bridges had remarkable handrails of black iron lace. But this was not enough for my father. He collected a hundred orb-web spiders and set them loose in the crevices and curlicues of the iron. Within the lace of the bridge, these spiders spun their own lace, and after a night of rain or dew the whole bridge glittered black and silver, spirals within spirals, an intricate piece of jewellery arching over a wide, stony stream.

People were enchanted with the unexpectedness of it. Now, as they crossed over, they became part of a work of art. But the same people certainly thought my father strange when he built another bridge of horsehair and vines so that rabbits, and even mice, could cross the river with dry feet and tails. He's gone all funny, they said, turning their mouths down. However, my father had only just begun. He made two bridges with gardens built into them which soon became so overgrown with roses, wisteria, bougainvillea and other beautiful climbing plants that they looked as if they had been made entirely of flowers.

Over a river that wound through a grove of silver birch trees he wove a bridge of golden wires, a great cage filled with brilliant, singing birds; and in a dull, tired town he made an aquarium bridge whose glass balustrades and parapets were streaked scarlet and gold by the fish that darted inside them. People began to go out of their way to cross my father's bridges.

Building surprising bridges was one thing, but soon my father took it into his head to build bridges in unexpected places. He gave up building them where people were known to be going and built them where people might happen to find themselves. Somewhere, far from any road, sliding through brush and ferns to reach a remote stretch of river, you might find one of my father's bridges: perhaps a strong one built to last a thousand years, perhaps a frail one made of bamboo canes, peacock feathers and violin strings. A bridge like this would soon fall to pieces sending its peacock feathers down the river like messages, sounding a single twangling note among the listening hills. Mystery became a part of crossing over by my father's bridges.

In some ways it seemed as if his ideas about what a bridge should be were changing. His next bridge, made of silver thread and mother of pearl, was only to be crossed at midnight on a moonlight night. So, crossing over changed, too. Those who crossed over from one bank to another on this bridge, crossed also from one day to another, crossing time as well as the spaces under the piers. It was his first time-bridge, but later there was to be another, a bridge set with clocks chiming perpetually the hours and half hours in other parts of the world. And in all the world this was the only bridge that needed to be wound up with a master key every eight days.

Wherever my father saw a promising space he thought of ways in which it could be crossed, and yet for all that he loved spaces. In the city he climbed like a spider, stringing blue suspension bridges between skyscrapers and tower blocks—air bridges, he called them. Looking up at them from the street they became invisible. When crossing over on them, you felt you were suspended in nothing, or were maybe set in crystal, a true inhabitant of the sky. Lying down, looking through the blue web that held you, you could see the world turning below. But if you chose to lie on your back and look up as far as you could look, and then a bit farther still, on and on, higher and higher, your eyes would travel through the troposphere and the tropopause, the stratosphere and stratopause, the mesosphere and the mesopause, the Heaviside layer, the ionosphere and the Appleton layer, not to mention the Van Allen belts. From my father's blue suspension bridges all the architecture of the air would open up to you.

However, not many people bothered to stare upwards like that. Only the true travellers were fascinated to realize that the space they carelessly passed through was not empty, but crowded with its own invisible constructions.

"Who wants a bridge like that, anyway?" some people asked sourly.

"Anyone. Someone!" my father answered. "There are no rules for crossing over."

But a lot of people disagreed with this idea of my

father's. Such people thought bridges were designed specially for cars, mere pieces of road stuck up on legs of iron or concrete, whereas my father thought bridges were the connections that would hold everything together. Bridges gone, perhaps the whole world would fall apart, like a quartered orange. The journey on the left bank of the river (according to my father) was quite different from the journey on the right. The man on the right bank of the ravine—was he truly the same man when he crossed on to the left? My father thought he might not be, and his bridges seemed like the steps of a dance which would enable the man with a bit of left-hand spin on him to spin in the opposite direction. This world (my father thought) was playing a great game called "Change," and his part in the game was called "crossing over."

It was upsetting for those people who wanted to stick to the road to know that some people used my father's hidden bridges. They wanted everyone to cross by exactly the same bridges that *they* used, and they hated the thought that, somewhere over the river they were crossing, there might be another strange and lovely bridge they were unaware of.

However, no one could cross all my father's bridges. No one can cross over in every way. Some people became angry when they realized this and, because they could not cross over on every bridge there was, they started insisting that there should be no more bridge building. Some of these people were very powerful—so powerful, indeed, that they passed laws forbidding my father to build any bridge unless ordered to do so by a government or by some county council. They might as well have passed a law saying that the tide was only allowed to come in and out by government decree, because by now my father's bridge building had become a force beyond the rule of law. He built another bridge, a secret one, which was not discovered until he had finished it, this time over a volcano. Its abutments were carved out of old lava and, along its side, great harps, instead of handrails, cast strange, striped shadows on the decking. Men, women and children who crossed over could look down into the glowing heart of the volcano, could watch it simmer and seethe and smoulder. And when the winds blew, or when the great fumes of hot air billowed up like dragon's breath, the harps played fiery music with no regard to harmony. This bridge gave the volcano a voice. It spoke an incandescent language, making the night echo with inexplicable songs and poetry.

"The bridge will melt when the volcano erupts," people said to each other, alarmed and fascinated by these anthems of fire.

"But none of my bridges are intended to last for ever," my father muttered to himself, loading his derrick and winch on to the back of his truck and driving off in another direction. It was just as well he kept on the move. Powerful enemies pursued him.

"Bridges are merely bits of the road with special problems," they told one another, and sent soldiers out to trap my father, to arrest him, to put an end to his bridge building. Of course, they couldn't catch him. They would think they had him cornered and, behold, he would build a bridge and escape—a bridge that collapsed behind him as if it had been made of playing cards, or a bridge that unexpectedly turned into a boat, carrying his astonished pursuers away down some swift river.

Just about then, as it happened, my travelling took me on my first circle around the world, and I wound up back where I had started from. My brother, the electrical engineer, and my sister, the doctor, came to see me camping under a bridge that my father had built when I was only three years old.

"Perhaps you can do something about him," Philippa cried. "He won't listen to us."

"Don't you care?" asked Simon. "It's a real embarrassment. It's time he was stopped before he brings terrible trouble upon himself."

They looked at me—shaggy and silent, with almost nothing to say to them—in amazement. I gave them the only answer I could.

"What is there for a bridge builder to build, if he isn't allowed to build bridges?" I asked them. Dust from the world's roads made my voice husky, even in my own ears.

"He can be a retired bridge builder," Simon replied. "But I can see that you're going to waste time asking riddles. You don't care that your old father is involved in illegal bridge building." And he went away. He had forgotten the weekend picnics in the sunshine, and the derrick, high as a ladder, leading to the stars.

"And what have you become, Merlin?" Philippa asked me. "What are you now, after all your journeys?"

"I'm a traveller as I always have been," I replied.

"You are a vagabond," she answered scornfully. "A vagabond with a magician's name, but no magic!"

Then she went away, too, in her expensive car. I did not tell her, but I did have a little bit of magic—a single magical word, half-learned, half-invented. I could see that my father might need help, even a vagabond's help, even the help of a single magic word. I set off to find him.

It was easy for me, a seasoned traveller, to fall in with my father. I just walked along, until I came to a river that sang his name, and then I followed that river up over slippery stones and waterfalls, through bright green tangles of cress and monkey musk. Sure enough, there was my father building a bridge by bending two tall trees over the water and plaiting the branches into steps. This bridge would, in time, grow leafy handrails filled with birds' nests, a crossing place for deer and possums.

"Hello!" said my father. "Hello, Merlin. I've just boiled the billy.[1] Care for a cup of tea?"

"Love one!" I said. "There's nothing quite like a cup of billy-tea." So we sat down in a patch of sunlight and drank our tea.

"They're catching up with me, you know," my father said sadly. "There are police and soldiers looking all the time. Helicopters, too! I can go on escaping, of course, but I'm not sure if I can be bothered. I'm getting pretty bored with it all. Besides," he went on, lowering his voice as if the green shadows might overhear him, "I'm not sure that building bridges is enough any longer. I feel I must become more involved, to cross over myself in some way. But how does a bridge builder learn to cross over when he's on both sides of the river to begin with?"

"I might be able to help," I said.

My father looked up from under the brim of his working hat. He was a weatherbeaten man, fingernails cracked by many years of bridge building. Sitting there, a cup of billy-tea between his hands, he looked like a tree, he looked like a rock. There was no moss on him, but he looked mossy for all that. He was as lined and wrinkled as if a map of all his journeys, backwards and forwards, were inscribed on his face, with crosses for all the bridges he had built.

"I'm not sure you can," he answered. "I must be *more* of a bridge builder not *less* of one, if you understand me."

"Choosy, aren't you?" I said, smiling, and he smiled back.

---

[1] **billy:** an Australian term for a metal pot or kettle used in camp cooking

"I suppose you think you know what I'd like most," he went on.

"I think I do!" I replied. "I've crossed a lot of bridges myself one way and another, because I'm a travelling man, and I've learned a lot on the banks of many rivers."

"And you've a magical name," my father reminded me eagerly. "I said, when you were born, this one is going to be the magician of the family!"

"I'm not a magician," I replied, "but there *is* one word I know . . . a word of release and remaking. It allows things to become their true selves." My father was silent for a moment, nodding slowly, eyes gleaming under wrinkled lids.

"Don't you think things are really what they seem to be?" he asked me.

"I think people are all, more or less, creatures of two sides with a chasm in between, so to speak. My magic word merely closes the chasm."

"A big job for one word," said my father.

"Well, it's a very good word," I said. I didn't tell him I had invented half of it myself. "It's a sort of bridge," I told him.

All the time we talked, we had felt the movement of men, not very close, not very far, as the forest carried news of my father's pursuers. Now we heard a sudden sharp cry—and another—and another. Men shouted in desperate voices.

"It's the soldiers," my father said, leaping to his feet. "They've been hunting me all day, though the forest is on my side and hides me away. But something's happened. We'd better go and check what's going on. I don't want them to come to harm because of me and my bridge-building habits."

We scrambled upstream until the river suddenly started to run more swiftly, narrow and deep. The opposite bank rose up sharply, red with crumbling, rotten rock, green with mosses and pockets of fern. My father struggled to keep up with me. He was old, and besides, he was a bridge builder, not a traveller. Closing my eyes for a moment against the distractions around me, I brought the magic word out of my mind and on to the tip of my tongue—and then I left it unspoken.

The soldiers were on the opposite bank. They had tried to climb down the cliff on rotten rock but it had broken away at their very toes and there they were, marooned on a crumbling ledge—three of them—weighted down with guns, ammunition belts and other military paraphernalia. Two of the soldiers were very young, and all three of them were afraid, faces pale, reflecting the green leaves greenly.

Below them the rocks rose out of the water. Just at this point the river became a dragon's mouth, full of black teeth, hissing and roaring, sending up a faint smoke of silver spray.

It was obvious that the soldiers needed a bridge.

My father stared at them, and they stared at him like men confounded. But he was a bridge builder before he was anybody's friend or enemy, before he was anybody's father.

"That word?" he asked me. "You have it there?"

I nodded. I dared not speak, or the word would be said too soon.

"When I step into the water, say it then, Merlin!"

I waited and my father smiled at me, shy and proud and mischievous all at once. He looked up once at the sky, pale blue and far, and then he stepped, one foot on land, one in the water, towards the opposite bank. I spoke the word.

My father changed before my eyes. He became a

bridge as he had known he would. As for the word—it whispered over the restless surface of the river and rang lightly on the red, rotten rock. But my father had taken its magic out of it. No one else was altered.

The curious thing was that my father, who had made so many strange and beautiful bridges, was a very ordinary-looking bridge himself—a single-span bridge built of stone over an arch of stone, springing upwards at an odd angle, vanishing into the cliff at the very feet of the terrified soldiers. He looked as if he had always been there, as if he would be there forever, silver moss on his handrails, on his abutments, even on his deck. Certainly he was the quietest bridge I had ever crossed as I went over to help the soldiers down. There was no way forward through the cliff. Still, perhaps the job of some rare bridges is to cross over only briefly and then bring us back to the place we started from.

We came back together, the three soldiers and I, and I'm sure we were all different men on the right bank from the men we had been on the left.

Our feet made no sound on the silver moss.

"They can say what they like about that old man," cried the older soldier all of a sudden, "but I was never so pleased to see a bridge in all my life. It just shows there are good reasons for having bridges in unexpected places."

Together we scrambled downstream and, at last, back on to the road.

"But who's going to build the bridges now, then?" asked one of the young soldiers. "Look! You were with him. Are you a bridge builder, too?"

They knew now. They knew that unexpected bridges would be needed.

But someone else will have to build them. I am not a bridge builder. I am a traveller. I set out travelling, after that, crossing, one by one, all the bridges my father had built . . . the picnic-bridges of childhood, the wooden ones, the steel ones, the stone and the concrete. I crossed the blue bridges of the air and those that seemed to be woven of vines and flowers. I crossed the silver-thread and mother-of-pearl bridge one moonlit midnight. I looked down into the melting heart of the world and saw my reflection in a bubble of fire while the harps sang and sighed and snarled around me with the very voice of the volcano.

Some day someone, perhaps my own child, may say that word of mine back to me—that word I said to my father—but I won't turn into a bridge. I shall become a journey winding over hills, across cities, along seashores and through shrouded forests, crossing my father's bridges and the bridges of other men, as well as all the infinitely divided roads and splintered pathways that lie between them.

The Basket

I
And that's how they make a basket—

With saskatoon wood,
Spruce roots
And thin cherry bark.

The saskatoon wood makes it strong.
The spruce roots make the weave.
The cherry bark is design.

The saskatoon,
The spruce
And the choke cherry tree.

II
It's made of birchbark, this one.
We use them for picking berries.
They're good for berry baskets.

First we cut the birchbark from the tree.
Don't just take any kind.
By the feel of it, yes, how thick—
You've got to pick it out.

Don't just cut it anyway.
You cut it toward the sun this way.
An old man told me "cut toward the sun."

See the dark brown bark lines how short they are.
Is good. The long lines tear.
The short are strong, just as God made them.

Don't just sew with anything.
Use the spruce root where it strings out
Just below the ground.

Take it up with gloves
and peel them and split them—
It's easy when the sap is running.

And make it strong with saskatoon wood.
Bent around the brim.
And put a handle on of buckskin.

And there you have a berry basket—
A birchbark berry basket.
Layer on layer, just as God made it.

MARY AUGUSTA TAPPAGE

A Man and His Flute

A man in a black coat
plays a song
on a black flute
in a concert hall.
He plays with his whole
body with his hands
with his trunk until
he becomes a tree and
his arm a branch;
his fingers are urgent
extensions that startle
the air in the leaves.

His song is obscurely
about a lemon
picked from an old tree
in another country then
brought home and cut
against the blue
of a winter sky.

The lemon and the
black flute and the man
in the black coat who
sways with the music
in the concert hall

takes the blue sky the
yellow lemon and the
cold sunlight of March
and turns it into an April
filled with the blueness
of hyacinth; winter turns
its back and melts away
in the runnelled snow piled
against frozen houses.

The man and his flute
play their song,
the audience is pierced
by the blueness of sky,
the audience hears
the snow melting,
the audience sees spring
approaching the audience
stands up the audience claps,
the audience dances.

The man and his flute
end their song,
a smell of cut lemon
fills the air.

MIRIAM WADDINGTON

The Spark

An essay by Phyllis Reynolds Naylor

"How, exactly," asked a friend, "do you *start* a book? What do you do first?"

There seems to be some idea that if writing could be reduced to steps one through ten, like a recipe, you could open the oven door at the end and take out a finished book. Or, at the very least, if you got off to a proper start, you could automatically follow through. That's the scary part about being a writer. There's no guarantee that, even if you put in a fifteen-hour day, you're going to accomplish anything at all.

If I were baking bread or weaving a rug, I would know when I got up in the morning that if I followed my instructions carefully, I would have something to show for it at the end of the day. I might be tired from having come home late the night before, or I might be worried about a member of my family, but the bread would be baked or the rug would be woven.

As a writer, however, I'm always conscious of the time when I go out for the evening. I know that if my mind is to function the next day, I have to be alert, and that if I am upset over something, it will be hard to concentrate. With every new book, there is an awful mixture of anticipation and terror; I am wildly excited by what I want to do, but there is absolutely no assurance that I will be able to do it. It doesn't matter how many books I have written or what prizes they might have won. A new book is always a gamble.

While one book may require only one handwritten draft before it goes onto the word processor, another may require many, many drafts in longhand before it ever gets to that stage. While working from an outline might be best for one story, another might do better with no outline at all. But even if the mechanics, the nitty-gritty of writing, were the same for all books and all authors, there is a certain spark that is necessary to bring a book to life, and that is the most difficult of all to explain.

I know, by an overwhelming feeling of excitement, when I'm ready to begin a new book. This is more than just thinking, Now that's a nice idea! There is a notebook beside my chair filled with book ideas—with plots and characters, even the entire outline, chapter by chapter, of a mystery—but for the moment, that's all they are: just ideas. At some point, however, after something I've read or something I've dreamed or something I remember from the past, I think, I could do something special with that idea! I see a way to bring a bit of myself to a plot, to contribute something that is uniquely mine. It's this that starts the excitement.

The Agony of Alice began to "grow" when I remembered, with embarrassment, playing Tarzan with a neighborhood boy when I was eight. I was Jane, and at some point in my script, he was supposed to kiss me. Although I wanted him to, I collapsed in embarrassment whenever he got within a foot of my face.

I began thinking of all the other things I had done as a young girl that were silly or stupid, and how fervently I hoped that whoever had seen me do them had either forgotten them by now or was dead. I knew, as most writers discover sooner or later, that whatever has happened to me—whatever I thought or felt, no matter how humiliating or unusual it seemed at the time—has usually happened to others as well. And so I became tremendously excited with the idea of a funny book about a girl named Alice and all the agonies she suffers when she remembers the embarrassing things that have happened to her. The book begins with Alice talking:

> The summer between fifth and sixth grades, something happens to your mind. With me, the box of Crayolas did it—thirty-two colors, including copper and burgundy. I was putting them in a sack for our move to Silver Spring when I remembered how I used to eat crayons in kindergarten.

> I didn't just eat them, either. One day when I was bored I stuck two crayons up my nostrils, then leaned over my desk and wagged my head from side to side like an elephant with tusks, and the teacher said, "Alice McKinley, what on earth are you doing?"

As a matter of fact, I never stuck crayons up my nose and wagged my head, but I saw a boy do it in third grade, and I remember thinking, Now that is the stupidest thing I have ever seen, and I'll remember it all my life. And I have. But it merely reminds me that maybe other people are remembering all the ridiculous things that *I've* done, and the only way to feel better about that is to laugh.

For some books, it takes a long time for the spark to kindle. Many years ago, I read a magazine article that said that the three most popular words in book titles for children are *horse, mystery,* and *secret.* Then the writer went on to say, tongue-in-cheek, that if an author wanted to write the all-time favorite children's book, he or she should call it "The Secret Mystery Horse." I filed this away in the back of my mind.

A few years after that, I thought about it again. Well, why *not?* I thought. Why not write a good mystery that involves a horse? The moment I thought about it, however, I knew why not: because I knew hardly a thing about horses. My only experience with them, other than seeing them from a distance on the farm, is that when I was a freshman in high school, I enrolled in a riding class that met on Saturday mornings. I didn't want to ride horses nearly as much as I wanted to wear jodhpurs like the rich girls who lived on the west side of town.

The first thing I discovered was that I looked terrible in jodhpurs. The next thing I discovered was that I was terrified of horses. Every week I went to that stable in a state of dread. And because I was content to take the horse slowly around the ring, the instructor would come over from time to time and hit the horse on its hindquarters with a switch, forcing it into a trot. I would cling to the mane and pray for deliverance. That was all I knew about horses. So I asked myself, Why not write about a girl, then, who is terrified of horses, or perhaps of a certain horse?

Now I was beginning to feel excited, because I could see myself in the story. There was still the problem of writing about horses when I didn't know much about them, and I realized that the only way I could handle this was to keep the horse very much in the background while still making it an important part of the book. I decided to do this by having the girl suspect the horse of being a demon.

I would hold this terror continually over the reader's head while conveniently keeping the horse itself safely behind the fence in the pasture. So much for the horse.

All the while the anticipation builds about a book-to-be, I am getting a sense of the mood of the story. I wanted to place this story somewhere that would contribute to a mood of loneliness and isolation.

My father and his people were from Mississippi. They weren't city people, but lived out in the backwoods. The trips we had taken to visit them clung to me over the years like the moss that hung on the trees, and now the story began to grow right before my eyes. I would place my characters in the hill country of northeastern Mississippi. The mood was complete when I decided that I would make the girl's father in the story a calendar salesman, as my own father had been for a time. Although my father was more sophisticated than Ellen April's in the book, I had met enough of his relatives over the years to feel very much at home with them, and could easily put myself in their little dogtrot cabin on five acres of land. At this point, I was ready to begin the book, to shape the plot, and I no longer cared about making it "an all-time favorite." Instead of "The Secret Mystery Horse," I called my book *Night Cry*. It begins:

> Fear, like icy pellets, rained down on her as Ellen entered the barn. In the sudden darkness she could not see him, but she knew that Sleet was there.

Any number of things can spark enthusiasm in me for an idea. It isn't always a character that excites me first, like Alice McKinley in *The Agony of Alice,* or the mood cast by the demon horse in *Night Cry*. Sometimes it is simply the situation. In *The Solomon System,* two brothers, Ted and Nory—who have always been very close—have to cope with the disintegration of their parents' marriage and their own growing apart. Because I had known several families in which the children seemed caught in the middle of the parents' quarrels, I knew that I could do something special with this idea. And sometimes the spark begins not with character or plot or situation or mood, but with a theme—the "message" or "meaning" of a book. The message of my young adult novel *Dark of the Tunnel,* for example, is that no matter who we are or where we live, there is something we can do to promote peace, to make our voices heard.

For me, a book seems rather pointless unless the main character changes in some way. This doesn't mean there will always be a happy ending. It doesn't even mean that the character need change for the better. But if nothing happens during the story that is different from any other time, and the protagonist is exactly the same at the end as he was at the beginning, the reader may well say, "So what?"

And so, when I start work on a new book, I know how it will begin, how it will end, and a few of the things that will happen along the way. I also have a good idea of what the climactic scene will be—the turning point in the plot, so to speak. In *Night Cry* it is Ellen's hair-raising rescue with the horse she once feared; in *The Keeper* it is Nick's realization that he must let go of his closely guarded secret.

Other than these specific guideposts, however, the rest of the plot is usually something of a mystery, as though I am walking through a maze. Sometimes I seem to be leading my characters and other times they are leading me, but if I try to make them do something that is not absolutely right for them, the writing becomes laborious and the magic goes out of the page. Then I have to stop, go back, and get in touch with them again.

When I first began writing, it was hard enough to put characters, a theme, and a plot together without trying to complicate them in any way. But half the fun of writing is to bring out several different sides of a personality and to weave subplots in and around the main plot, tying them together in the end. Much as Ted and Nory like each other in *The Solomon System*, Ted's childishness often gets on Nory's nerves, and Nory, in turn, can be sullen and uncommunicative. And while the main plot in *Night Cry* is the kidnapping and rescue, there are subplots of gossip in the small mountain community and what it can lead to, of the retarded boy's struggle for acceptance, and of Ellen's need to break out of her shyness and experience more of the world. The deeper I dig into my story, the more I enjoy writing it.

It would be so much easier if book ideas came to me in an orderly fashion, each one waiting its turn. Some of them do. But others descend on me in a hurry, upsetting and exhilarating me, both at the same time. They push their way ahead of the rest, demand to be recognized, and make whatever book I'm working on at the time seem insignificant.

It's always been hard for me to keep my mind on the book at hand. There are a stack of three-ring notebooks by my chair, each filled with notes and clippings for a book-to-be, and I'm sure that on my deathbed I will gasp, "But I still have five more books to write!"

Monica **Hughes**

An interview by Gillian O'Reilly

Winner of numerous awards for her novels (Writing for Young People Contest, the Beaver Award, The Vicky Metcalfe Award), Hughes has also won the Canada Council Children's Literature Award twice—in 1982 for The Keeper of the Isis Light *and in 1983 for* The Guardian of Isis.

Gillian O'Reilly: Did you always want to be a writer?
Monica Hughes: Yes, since I was about ten. It was a dream, but not a dream that I ever worked at. It wasn't until about 12 years ago that I decided to sit down and make a commitment to myself to work at being a writer for a year, writing four hours a day. If that didn't work, I'd forget this whole dream and go and work in a store or something like that.

Did you do any writing when you were young?
At age ten it was a dream, nothing else. But in the

growing up years we did an awful lot of verse, essays and compositions in the schools. I tried my hand as an adult at writing articles, but didn't like it. I also wrote a couple of unsuccessful adult novels. And finally came to what I write now.

Did you read a lot when you were young?

A tremendous amount—high adventure and science fiction when I was young; later on, fantasy. In the class library at a school I went to in England were the works of E. Nesbit—wonderful books—and that gave me a great love of fantasy that has stayed with me ever since. It's still one of my favorite forms of reading, even though I don't write fantasy.

When you decided to try writing for a year, did you set out to write for young people?

It happened in a roundabout way. I went to the library one day and found a book called *Writing for the Juvenile and Teenage Market,* quite a good book. I just borrowed it out of interest. I love new books, and it was on the shelf among all the brand new, untouched books. While reading it I started getting quite excited. I went back to the library and read the various books of critical essays that the writer had suggested you tackle first. Of the enormous bibliography I read all the top books that she suggested and I realized what wonderful stuff was being written—much better than when I was growing up! In my childhood it was all about school adventures: midnight feasts and rivalries between gangs—dreadful stuff. The work I now discovered was literature, real literature. So when I made the choice to write for a year, it was with the idea of aiming towards the quality of these writers, these great lights in the sky.

Which writers did you discover?

I discovered Rosemary Sutcliffe, Alan Garner, Leon

Garfield, Penelope Farmer, Penelope Lively, Philippa Pearce, a whole range of classics—wonderful stuff. And you know, I still read them.

Why did you choose to write science fiction?

By chance, I didn't pick it, it picked me. I happened to turn on the TV after I had struggled my way through two adventure novels, which were not good. I found a Jacques Cousteau program about an underwater habitat in the Red Sea. So I started imagining a whole city under water and what it would be like for kids to grow up there. I thought, "How exciting, this is what I want to write about." Of course, to answer the question about what it would be like to be a kid growing up under the sea, you have to be writing science fiction. And that was how, by chance, I literally fell into it.

You also have to think about what it is like to be a child growing up. Do you find that hard to do?

I'm thinking particularly of characters like the 16-year-old boy in Hunter in the Dark.

I don't know how close I am to reality, but it doesn't seem difficult to remember. I become the person and the age that I'm writing about. You get inside the character's skin and you think as he does, and you lose your own self-consciousness, as it were, rather like an actor.

You've also written one historical novel and some present-day fiction.

The historical work was about kids going through the first winter of the Klondike Gold Rush, 1897-98. I was asked to do it as a commission from an Edmonton publisher, so with some trepidation I did the research and wrote it. *Hunter in the Dark, The Ghost Dance Caper,* and *The Treasure of the Long Sault,* are set in today's world, because the question I wanted to look at in each story could only be answered in today's world. There's no point in going to the future just for the sake of doing it. I could have made the hunter (in *Hunter in the Dark*) to be a hunter of some strange alien beast from some other planet, but it wouldn't have spoken to the reader in the way I wanted it to.

Yet, science fiction is your favorite medium?

It's where I belong, unless an idea comes so strongly to me that I have to take it. I forget a lot of ideas because they turned out to be not what I wanted.

Do you feel that science fiction is important for young people to read?

I do think so . . . for several reasons. I think it is in a way the mythology of today. The anthropologist Claude Levi-Strauss said that mythology was primitive man's way of making this frightening world explicable. He didn't understand any of the rules: Why is there lightning and thunder? What are earthquakes? Why do people die? So he turned to mythology to make it explicit and bearable. Well, now we're coming into a very new world, this electronic micro-chip world, and I think we need a kind of mythology to make us feel comfortable and learn to live with it.

Now, the second thing is: I am very much afraid that we are accepting this new world unquestioningly. "Is this the right choice?", "Are we doing this for the right reason?" I like people to ask questions within my stories. This is why they are very often open-ended. You have to remember that we are human beings, and it is not necessarily a great thing to turn our world into a structure that is comfortable for computers to live in. We are already experiencing difficulties. We have to learn, for instance, the way computers write numerals and letters; they're not going to change and write cursive. I think that will continue: we adapt to the computer, not it to us. I ask questions about that.

Your stories are often open-ended.

Some of the kids hate that. They say, "When are you going to write a sequel to so-and-so?" With *Ring-Rise, Ring-Set,* they want to find out whether the Tech scientists did push the glacier back and what happened to Liza. I don't know. I think that the Techs are going to have an incredibly difficult choice and I don't know which one they make.

Where do your ideas come from?

Everywhere. Something comes to me in the form of a question and I don't know the answer to it, so I seek it out. The one I've just finished is called *Devil on my Back.* It was an idea I picked up from the *En Route* magazine on an Air Canada flight. There were a lot of articles on computer technology and one of the authors went out on a limb and suggested that, in the future, perhaps we might have micro-processors attached to our own bodies. My question is, of course, what kind of society would use micro-processors in this way and how would it turn out? And this gave us *Devil on my Back.* You can gather from the title that I'm not crazy about the notion myself.

How do you do your research?

Mostly in the public library and I go there with an open mind. I'm writing a book about deserts now. I know the title and one minor character. I have no idea what's going to happen so I'm just going down to the library, looking in the shelves and the periodical section for articles about deserts. Things happen and it all comes together. The search area often leads to the story.

You write every day from 8 A.M. till noon. That must take a lot of discipline.

I think it would take more discipline to be a writer if you didn't have regular hours. It's much simpler to tell yourself that you work from 8 to 12 as if you had a regular job.

What happens if you get a block at 10:00?

I walk around and scream and pull my hair out. It's O.K. when I'm alone. It is always resolved in the end. I may find that there's a question missing in my research and the reason I'm blocked is because I'm going into unknown territory. So, I have to go back and find out a little bit more about the subject.

Are there novels you've started and didn't finish?

Only one in the beginning. I started to write a sequel to *Crisis on Conshelf Ten* and *Earthdark*. I wasn't crazy about doing it, but I thought it would sell well. Suddenly, I came across a book with an almost identical plot, so I just happily tore mine up and threw it away.

How long does it take you to write a book from start to finish?

Anywhere from three months, which is the dead shortest, to about six months. I try to write two books a year.

You once said you considered yourself a part-time writer.

I consider it full-time now. Tours, talks and things like that take up time and I have a lot of correspondence. Then, of course, there is the thinking process. Very often, it is going on for most of the day; you don't cut that off.

Do you still do weaving?

I've had to give that up because of lack of time. I have two looms gathering dust.

Did you ever work weaving into one of your stories?

One story that never sold. It was very bad. I was writing very self-consciously as I tried to include the idea of spinning and weaving.

Your biographical notes say that you've lived in many places in Britain, Canada and Africa. Has the ability to adjust to new places had an influence on your writing?

I think so, very much. Because I'm rootless I don't write about my antecedents. I've had to go out on a limb into space, because I can't make connections any other way.

Someone pointed out that all my heroes go on journeys. This is true, but think about myths and sagas, those heroes all go on journeys. Life is a journey. It must be very difficult to write this kind of book if you've lived all your life in the same place.

Your heroes are very often individuals who escape from very structured, traditional roles. Is this a conscious choice?

Very often a satisfactory protagonist is somewhat of a rebel. It's difficult to make exciting heroes out of people who are perfectly contented with their lot. If they are rebels living in a perfectly nice society, they become somewhat obnoxious. So I tend to make the societies rather restrictive to make the characters more sympathetic. It's probably just as simple as that.

Girl with 'Cello

There had been no such music here until
A girl came in from falling dark and snow
To bring into this house her glowing 'cello
As if some silent, magic animal.

She sat, head bent, her long hair all aspill
Over the breathing wood, and drew the bow.
There had been no such music here until
A girl came in from falling dark and snow.

And she drew out that sound so like a wail,
A rich dark suffering joy, as if to show
All that a wrist holds and that fingers know
When they caress a magic animal.
There had been no such music here until
A girl came in from falling dark and snow.

MAY SARTON

Roots

A short story by Eric Cameron

Sultry weather and the swaying of the train made Edouard Tourville's head droop. His wife, Marie-Anne, dozed beside him. The tiny, gentle-voiced woman had seldom left the village during her more than sixty years there.

When their Spartan existence on the small farm drove their only son, Paul, to the city, Marie-Anne counted the months like beads on her rosary for his return. But Paul had joined the Air Force and married just before the terrible flying accident that took his life. Because his attractive wife was an orphan, the Tourvilles brought her to live with them. Tragedy had struck again and two days after her baby boy was christened Marcel, the Tourvilles buried Paul's widow.

"You have God's finest gift to console you," the village priest assured them. "A sturdy grandson who will inherit your farm, the land his father scorned."

Marcel had his father's wavy black hair and high spirits, and his mother's love of beautiful things. But at sixteen, Marie-Anne would find Marcel brooding, plagued by some gnawing discontent. He had taken to drawing on almost every clean surface he could find. Edouard had been amused, then puzzled, finally irritated. Then Marcel's unexpected request to be sent to study at a school in Montreal was the climax. As headstrong as his father, he finally left, leaving his grandparents feeling that something in their lives had been extinguished.

The train's jolting woke Marie-Anne and Edouard. She reread Marcel's note about the art school's display of student work.

The school's reception hall was crowded. Long-haired, bearded young men in casual clothing mingled with pale-faced girls whose hair was cut in boyish style or hung to their waists. Marcel had sprouted a weedy moustache and his hair needed cutting. Before they could say more than a few words of greeting, the hum of conversation died.

"They're announcing the awards and scholarships," whispered a slender, flaxen-haired girl beside Marcel.

Marie-Anne and Edouard listened but understood little, applauding when others did. Then Marcel was announced as the winner of a special bursary.

"Terrific!" he exclaimed. "I can continue my work in *Paris!*"

Edouard groaned. "You don't have to pay," Marcel explained. "The bursary covers everything. But because I'm not quite eighteen, I'll need your permission."

Marie-Anne's work-worn hands in gray gloves fluttered like apprehensive doves. Edouard tugged at his ear. "You can go," he said gruffly, turned and pretended to study an abstract painting he couldn't really see because of tears. Marie-Anne tugged his sleeve. "What about the paintings for Father Benoit?"

"Decorations for a country church won't mean anything to him now," Edouard muttered.

When Marie-Anne looked for Marcel, he was whispering urgently to the girl with a face like an angel in some ancient fresco. Marie-Anne shyly handed Marcel a slim, leather-bound volume wrapped in green tissue salvaged from Christmas. "I—I thought you'd like to keep this . . . a—a souvenir of happy times," she murmured, then hurried away after Edouard. "We'll be back after looking at the exhibition," she called, although she knew Edouard had no intention of remaining.

Marcel leafed through the collection of his early sketches. Each little scene capsuled an hour, a day, an experience. The girl exclaimed in delight at a sparkling pastel of the steep-gabled house where he had been born. Marcel remembered the diamond-bright glitter of the fresh snow that day . . . the way the sleigh bells had tinkled like slivers of crystal.

Looking up, he found himself the center of a group of students appraising his sketches. One of his instructors was among them.

"You should have let me see those the first day you came here," the middle-aged teacher said.

"Why?"

"Because I think you're a true primitive painter. You express yourself best in an informal technique. Who knows, if you go to Paris you might be making a mistake."

"A *mistake?*"

The teacher nodded. "Your earliest work indicates a strong, fresh approach. The style has striking individuality. Remember, individuality of outlook and expression are the marks of true creative artists." He shrugged. "But, it's entirely up to you to decide."

During the melancholy return journey, Marie-Anne managed to coax Edouard into stopping off at the shrine of Ste. Anne de Beaupré. She was worried that if he returned immediately to the farm he would sink into bitter silence and depression. By pretending that she was faint from the heat and excitement, she persuaded Edouard to rent a room in a small hotel.

After a week, Edouard regained so much energy he complained about the mattress, the skimpiness of the meals, the traffic and tourists. Then Marie-Anne knew it was safe to continue home.

As the village's only taxi whisked them past the old houses, the Tourvilles sensed their arrival was noticed by many people. Marie-Anne had an uneasy feeling that the taxi driver's silence was deliberate.

"I think I'll paint the barn this week," Edouard remarked.

When the driver's head jerked around for a startled look, Edouard barked at him to watch the road.

The old barn struck them first. The side facing the road had been transformed into a huge, semi-abstract mural. Figures of epic proportions symbolized in an eye-catching way elements of rural life. The effect was like a great stained-glass window. Several cars were stopped by the fence, their occupants staring at the barn. As Edouard and Marie-Anne stood speechless by their old stone farmhouse, the door opened and Marcel hurried out. His work pants and shirt were spattered with many colors of paint. His eyes sparkled.

"How do you like it?"

For once, Edouard was completely at a loss for words. Marie-Anne's dark eyes brimmed as she embraced Marcel.

"I got the idea after you left the school," he told his grandparents. "Why spend the bursary money in Paris when I could do something exciting right here."

Edouard gulped. "Do what?"

"We're going to put this place on the map!" Marcel exclaimed. Eight of his fellow students emerged from the barn, including the girl with the angelic face. "This summer we'll have an art and handicrafts festival," Marcel explained. "There's room in the barn for a studio and the group will pay for their meals. Just think! Tourists will stop to look at that big mural on the barn, then they'll buy paintings on display. Plus hooked rugs, antiques, wood carvings!"

"You mean you're home to stay?" Edouard asked.

"For good!" Marcel exclaimed. "My good. Everybody's good. My art teacher was right. Artists are like flowers; each flourishes best in his native soil. And *my* roots are right here."

Marie-Anne hugged him and, over his shoulder, whispered to Edouard. "At the shrine, I prayed to good Ste. Anne for help. I never expected a miracle!"

He tugged at his ear. "Remember how I used to be a pretty good wood-carver when I was young? No artist, mind you, but—"

"I can see you now," exclaimed Marcel, "in a rocker by the art display, whittling while the tourists watch."

"What a little schemer you are!" his grandmother laughed.

My **Left** Foot

From the autobiography
by Christy Brown

I was now ten and a half and beginning to sink deeper and deeper into myself. Mother tried, but nothing could rouse me, nothing could bring back the happy child that used to be me. He didn't exist any more. In his place was a tense, silent, great-eyed creature who had nerves as sharp as broken glass and as taut as telegraph wires.

Then, one Christmas, one of us—I think it was Paddy—got a box of paints from Santa Claus. That same year I got a box of toy soldiers, but the moment I saw Paddy's paints with all the wonderful colours and the long, slender fuzzy-haired brush I fell in love with them at once. I felt I must have them to keep as my own. I was fascinated by the little solid blocks of paint—blue, red, yellow, green and white. Later in the day I sat and watched Paddy as he tried to make some impression with the paints on a piece of white cardboard torn from an old shoe box, but he only made a mess and in a queer way I felt annoyed with him—and a bit jealous.

"Blow—I can't use these things!" he grumbled, flinging his brush down. "They're only for girls."

I saw my chance. Pushing out my box of lead soldiers towards him with my foot, I asked him, in grunts, to 'swop' them for his paints.

"Done!" exclaimed Paddy, glad to get rid of such a sissy's toy. "But how are you going to use them?"

I didn't know that myself, but I just lifted my left foot and smiled.

I put them away till all the excitement of Christmas was past. Then one quiet afternoon when there was nobody in the kitchen but mother and myself I crawled over to the press, opened the door with my foot and took the little black box of paints out and laid it on the floor in front of me.

"What are you up to?" said mother, coming over to where I squatted with my back against the wall. "Surely you're not trying to paint!"

I nodded very solemnly. I picked up the brush between my toes, wetted it in my mouth, then rubbed it on one of the paint squares—the bright blue one which I liked best. I next rubbed the brush against my other foot—and saw a blue spot on it when I took it away.

"It works!" I managed to exclaim, and I could feel my face hot with excitement.

"I'll get you water," said mother, going into the pantry and coming back with a cupful which she put on the floor beside me.

I had no paper. Mother got me some by tearing a page out of Peter's sum-copy. I dipped the brush into the water and rubbed on some vivid red paint. Then I steadied my foot and, while mother looked on intently, painted on the open page before me—the outline of a cross.

I grinned triumphantly up at her. I remembered how, on that day five years previously, we had sat together on the floor, almost in the same spot, while I shook and sweated as I drew with my left foot for the first time. Mother had been there at my side then—she was at my side now, still inspiring me onwards.

There was no sweating or shaking this time. I did it quite smoothly. I was holding a painting brush now, not a broken piece of chalk. But it meant the same thing—I had discovered a new way to communicate with the outside world, a new way to talk with my left foot.

As time went on I became more and more devoted to my little box of paints. I painted all sorts of crazy things, from a sketch of Peter's face—to which he indignantly objected—to a bunch of dead fish lying in the dustbin, done before Tibby the cat from next door finished them off.

Then mother managed to buy me some more paints and brushes, along with one or two drawing books and a pencil. This, of course, broadened my range of expression and allowed me to have a greater choice of subject. After the first few weeks of uncertainty and awkwardness, I settled down contentedly with my new pastime. I painted every day upstairs in the back bedroom, completely by myself.

I was changing. I didn't know it then, but I had found a way to be happy again and to forget some of the things that had made me unhappy. Above all I learned to forget myself. I didn't miss going out with my brothers now, for I had something to keep my mind active, something to make each day, a thing to look forward to.

I would sit crouched on the floor for hours, holding the brush between my toes, my right leg curled up under my left, my arms held tightly at my sides, the hands clenched. All my paints and brushes were around me, and I would get mother or father to pin the drawing paper to the floor with tacks to keep it steady. It looked a very queer awkward position, with my head almost between my knees and my back as crooked as a corkscrew. But I painted all my best pictures in this way, with the wooden floor as my only easel.

Slowly I began to lose my early depression. I had a feeling of pure joy while I painted, a feeling I had never experienced before and which seemed almost to lift me above myself. It was only when I wasn't painting that I became depressed and cross with everyone at home. At first mother thought she was doing the right thing in encouraging me to paint, thinking it would give me less time to become unhappy. But after a while she began to worry, because I was spending so much time alone. I'd sit for hours painting in the bedroom upstairs, unconscious of everything—including myself.

She often came up the stairs to see if I wanted any-thing, coming on tip-toe into the room. There she'd find me, bent over a picture, the brush in my toes. Sometimes she'd come over to brush the hair out of my eyes and wipe the sweat from my forehead, for although I could now use my left foot as easily as Peter or Paddy could use their hands, it was still a terrific strain on the rest of my body to sit on the floor crouched over a picture for almost the whole day. But often when mother came up to see if I was all right, I'd just nod my head curtly and grunt.

Theodate, *the* Different

A profile by Mary Evans Andrews

"Effie, Effie! Still in your school dress?"

Eight-year-old Effie looked up from her drawing as her beautiful mother entered the playroom. "Hurry, now. Our guests will soon be here. Iris will help you dress and bring you down for tea."

"Oh, Mama, do I have to?"

Effie's parents were tall and handsome. She was short, plump, and "plain." When they met her, most grownups would look surprised and politely admire her expensive dresses. Then they talked to each other while she stood by, feeling awkward and bored.

"Please come see what I'm drawing, Mama. It's my biggest house yet."

With a sigh, Effie's mother stepped over to her desk.

"It's very nice, dear. But you mustn't spend all your time drawing houses. You should be wearing your pretty clothes and going to parties like other girls."

In 1868, when Effie was born, proper young ladies grew up to be wives and mothers. Her parents could not believe their only child would want to do anything else. Effie's father was a millionaire; her mother, a popular and stylish society leader.

Growing up in a large Cleveland house, Effie was surrounded by servants—and she was lonely. The place she liked best was her grandmother's house in Salem, Ohio. There she could play with her cousins and even slide down the banisters. She wrote:

> Christmas morning: cousins laughing in the upstairs hall, legs thrown over the mahogany stair rail. Swish, and I am caught in the curve of the newel post. Tree and gifts wait inside the library. Its locked door refuses to open to determined rattling. Run to see the new snow through four-colored glass of the entry door. Blue makes a ghastly dawn, rose a cheery pink morning. Climbing on a chair, we see a golden world, and stretching on tiptoe, a violent red one.

When Effie was eight, she gave her parents a "portfolio" of her best drawings. Watching nervously, hoping for "expressions of delight," she received only halfhearted thank-yous.

At school, shy Effie was only interested in art and reading and didn't enjoy her classmates' games. Her rich parents traveled a lot, so she had plenty of time to read— and think. She decided that Effie was no name for a future architect. In fact it sounded downright silly. She changed her name to that of her grandmother, Theodate (which means "God's gift" or "God-given"). From that day, she refused to answer anyone who called her Effie.

Luckily, Theodate and her favorite cousin, Elizabeth, were sent off to boarding school together. It was the famous Miss Porter's School in Farmington, Connecticut. Theodate loved the charming little town with its beautiful old homes. Privately, she resolved to live *here,* not in crowded, busy Cleveland.

Of course, her parents had other plans. When she graduated, they took her on a "grand tour" of Europe. Theodate was thrilled by the beauty of foreign art and architecture. She sketched buildings everywhere, especially in England. The sturdy stone villages in the Cotswolds near London made a lasting impression on her. She knew that she would enjoy building houses more than anything.

Back in Cleveland, Mrs. Pope made an effort to launch her daughter into the social whirl. Theodate loved her parents, so she tried to please them—briefly. But going to parties dressed in Paris finery simply bored her to death.

Finally, she persuaded them to let her return to Farmington. She had a place picked out, a modest eighteenth century house. "They thought I would be tired of it in three months," she wrote later. "How wrong they were."

The old house needed repairs. She bought it and a cottage next-door, which she attached to the big house. Restoring them both, inside and out, was her first experience as a builder. Working on the house only made Theodate more interested in buildings. She realized that to use her imagination and creativity fully, repairing and restoring was not enough. She was determined to become a professional architect.

She decided to study at Princeton, though the school did not admit women. Theodate solved this problem by moving to the town and employing university professors as her private tutors. She was allowed to sit in on some classes in architecture, but she wasn't given college credit. Theodate didn't mind. All she wanted was information—to pass the exam for her architect's license.

Besides classroom study, Theodate knew she needed experience with an established architect. She convinced her parents to move to Farmington, and she began to design a large country house for them.

McKim, Mead and White, the largest architectural firm in New York in 1898, was hired to provide the drawings for the house. Theodate worked closely with the firm, and her ideas influenced the final design.

Theodate was interested in creating a new sort of house, one that looked original. She wanted it to remind people of their American background; she wanted it to be comfortable and homey, yet stand tall and proud. She used George Washington's Mount Vernon home as a model. Theodate's house was called Hill-Stead. One famous guest, Theodore Roosevelt, commented, "Hill-Stead is the ideal of what an American country home should be."

Theodate passed her architect's exam in 1910. Her first large job was to design a girl's school in Middlebury, Connecticut. Finished in 1912, the original building forms a handsome quadrangle, or hollow square. Students can walk from their rooms to classes, to meals, chapel, or library without going out in bad weather. Today, Westover School still stands, a boarding high school.

Mary Hillard, Theodate's good friend, was the new school's first headmistress. Theodate used to visit several times a year, sometimes without warning. Whenever "The Yellow Peril," her big, powerful sports car, roared up the drive, Miss Hillard would dismiss classes for the rest of the day. The girls were delighted.

In 1918 Theodate became a distinguished member of the American Institute of Architects. The Theodore Roosevelt Memorial Association chose her to rebuild the former president's birthplace in New York City. The townhouse had been torn down, and she had to start over from the original plans. She also had to add a wing to serve as a museum, and refurnish the home in the style of 1865.

When the National Park Service took over and spruced up the house more than fifty years later, they discovered how accurate she had been. Every detail down to the nails and cupboard hinges belonged to the correct period.

Theodate and her husband, the American diplomat John Wallace Riddle, had no children, but they raised three boys whose parents, all missionaries, had died. Perhaps because she had been so lonely and "different" as a child, Theodate always sympathized with young people. She would listen by the hour to their hopes and problems. "Be yourself," she advised. "Let the world think what it likes."

About the Authors

Mary Evans Andrews has lectured extensively on books and writing techniques. She has contributed many articles to adults' and children's magazines. Her interests include recorded music and hiking.

Christy Brown (1933–1981) was an Irishman who overcame cerebral palsy to write a best-selling novel about life in Dublin, *Down All the Days*. His life story is told in the award-winning film *My Left Foot*.

Eric Cameron has written many short stories which have been published in Canada and the United States. Some of his stories have been broadcast on the radio.

Banesh Hoffmann (1906–1986) became friends with Albert Einstein at Princeton University, where the two men worked together. Hoffmann, a writer and a mathematician, wrote two books about Einstein.

Robert Lipsyte has written several books for young adults, including *Jock and Jill, One Fat Summer,* and *Summerboy*. Before turning his talents to fiction, Lipsyte was an award-winning sportswriter for the *New York Times*. In addition to writing for young adults, he has also written screenplays and television scripts.

Margaret Mahy is a New Zealander who has written many short stories and several award-winning books for young adults. *The Changeover* was chosen by the American Library Association as one of the best books of 1984. Mahy has also written several classic picture books for very young readers.

Rick McNair was born in Amherst, Nova Scotia, in 1941. He has written more than thirty plays for adult and young audiences and has worked as artistic director of Theatre Calgary.

Phyllis Reynolds Naylor was born in 1933 and has written many essays and novels. She has been a full-time writer since 1960 and has been active in civil rights and peace organizations for many years.

Zibby Oneal says she always wanted to be a writer. She grew up in a house full of books and paintings and began to write for children when her own children were young. She now teaches literature and creative writing in Michigan.

Gillian O'Reilly was born in Montréal in 1956. She now lives in Toronto, where she works as a freelance journalist and editor.

May Sarton, who was born in 1912, has written forty-six books over the last fifty years, including poetry, fiction, and autobiography. Her poetry has recently been collected in *Selected Poems of May Sarton*. She currently lives in Maine.

Raymond Souster was born in Toronto in 1921 and has spent most of his adult life as a poet. His collection of poems entitled *The Colour of the Times* won him the Governor General's Award in 1964. Souster has also written a couple of novels under the pseudonyms Raymond Holmes and John Holmes.

Mary Augusta Tappage was born in 1888 at Soda Creek in the Cariboo region of British Columbia. Her grandfather was a Shuswap chief who moved west after the Riel Rebellion. Tappage's poems have been collected in a book entitled *The Days of Augusta*.

Mary Alice Thompson's short story "How Elsa Became an Artist" was originally published in the *Canadian Children's Annual 1988*, a collection of stories, articles, poems, games, cartoons, and illustrations for children.

Miriam Waddington was born in Winnipeg in 1917. She has written a dozen books of poetry, including *The Glass Trumpet, The Price of Gold,* and *Collected Poems.* Her poems have been translated and published in the former Soviet Union, France, Greece, Hungary, Japan, Romania, South America, and China.

Margaret Walker is a poet and novelist born in Birmingham, Alabama, in 1915. She has taught English literature at Jackson State College in Jackson, Mississippi, since 1949.

Diana J. Wieler has been a gifted storyteller ever since childhood. She received constant support for her creative efforts from her mother. Diana says, "We were always encouraged to make things, no matter the mess." In addition to writing many short stories, she has also written a novel entitled *Last Chance Summer.*

Elizabeth Yates, born in 1905, has won many awards for her children's books. She has written several books about historical figures, including *Prudence Crandall: Woman of Courage* and *Amos Fortune: Free Man.*

Jane Yolen was born in New York in 1939. She has written dozens of books for children and young adults. She enjoys folk music and dancing and describes herself as a "poet turned fantasist."

Credits

Grateful acknowledgment is given to authors, publishers, and agents for permission to reprint the following copyrighted material. Every effort has been made to determine copyright owners. In the case of any omissions, the Publisher will be pleased to make suitable acknowledgments in future editions.

1 From *Canadian Children's Annual*. Copyright © 1987 by John Street Press. Published by John Street Press.

6 Appeared in *Inquiry into Literature 3*, edited by Bryant Fillion and Jim Henderson. Copyright © 1981 by Collier Macmillan Canada, Inc. Published by Collier Macmillan Canada, Inc.

7 Appeared in *Sixteen*, edited by Donald R. Gallo. Copyright © 1984 by Robert Lipsyte. Published by Delacorte Press.

18 From *Canadian Children's Annual*. Copyright © 1988 by Grolier Limited. Published by Overlea House.

31 From *In Summer Light* by Zibby Oneal. Copyright © 1985 by Zibby Oneal. Published by Viking Kestrel.

37 From "Unforgettable Albert Einstein" by Banesh Hoffmann. Reprinted with permission from the January 1968 *Reader's Digest*. Copyright © 1967 by The Reader's Digest Assn., Inc.

44 Reprinted with permission of the author, c/o Playwrights Union of Canada, 54 Wolseley Street, Second Floor, Toronto, Ontario M5T 1A5.

67 From *The Writer on Her Work*, edited by Janet Sternburg. Copyright © 1980 by Janet Sternburg. Published by W. W. Norton & Company.

71 From *Dream Weaver* by Jane Yolen. Copyright © 1978 by Jane Yolen. Published by William Collins Publishers, Inc.

79 From "Under the Little Fir" by Elizabeth Yates. Copyright © 1942 by Elizabeth Yates. Published by Coward McCann Inc.

88 From *The Door in the Air* by Margaret Mahy. Copyright © 1976, 1988 by Margaret Mahy. Published by J. M. Dent & Sons Ltd.

100 From *The Days of Augusta*. Copyright © 1977 by David Day and Marilyn Bowering. Published by J. J. Douglas Ltd.

102 From The *Last Landscape* by Miriam Waddington. Copyright © 1992 by Miriam Waddington. Published by Oxford University Press.

104 From *How I Came to be a Writer* by Phyllis Reynolds Naylor. Copyright © 1978, 1987 by Phyllis Reynolds Naylor. Reprinted by permission of Aladdin Books, an imprint of Macmillan Publishing Company.

111 Appeared in *Jam* magazine, June 1984.

118 From *Collected Poems (1930–1973)* by May Sarton. Copyright © 1974 by May Sarton. Reprinted by permission of W. W. Norton & Company, Inc., and Russell and Volkening, Inc.

119 Appeared in *Short Story International,* Volume 16, Number 94, October 1992. Copyright © 1991 by Eric Cameron. Reprinted by permission of Short Story International, Great Neck, New York.

124 From *My Left Foot* by Christy Brown. Copyright © 1954 by Christy Brown. Published by Mandarin Paperbacks, The Octopus Publishing Group.

128 Appeared in *Cricket* magazine, Volume 18, Number 10, June 1991.